# WALKING CONTRADICTION

## THE CRACKPOT CHRONICLES

# MARISA TELLEZ

SECOND EDITION

Printed in the United States of America

Published by Pepperland Publishing

Cover Design by Casey Quintal

ISBN-10: 0988648121

ISBN-13: 978-0-9886481-2-8

# PERMISSIONS

Grateful acknowledgment is made for permission to reprint from the following:

# CONTENTS

1 I Heart New York!                              9

2 It Always Comes in Three's                    47

3 Emotional Limbo and More Arrests              65

4 Making Amends and the TV Star               103

5 The Wacky World of Television                135

6 My Biological Clock is Set to Snooze         167

7 Making Lemons Into Lemonade                  193

8 Epilogue                                     205

*This book is dedicated to my hometown of Los Angeles. No other city has brought me more heartbreak, stress, love, and opportunity. I can't imagine living anywhere else. There's no place like home.*

*I also dedicate this book to my father, Oscar "Duffy" Tellez who is now parted from me. Thank you for your unconditional love, endless knowledge of power tools, and your service in the military.*
*I miss you every single day. I hope I make you proud.*

# 1

# I HEART NEW YORK!

*I*t was the morning after my 20th birthday party. My mom dropped something on the living room floor that scared me out of my sleep. I woke up flailing my arms like a wild gorilla and knocked over a glass of water that was sitting on my nightstand. I had no plans to get out of bed and clean it up anytime soon. I was incredibly hung over.

This was more than the traditional household hangover. I thought about the events from the night before and the last years of my life that were spent partying on the Sunset Strip. Was it a crazy, lucid dream or did all of it really happen?

I also thought about how I screwed up my friendship with Cassidy and the girls by letting my feelings for Dresden get in the way. Yes Dresden. My supposed "first love". The man who broke my heart for a second time and ruined my birthday party before cowering back to New York.

I repeatedly told myself it was a bad dream. None of it ever happened. I sat up in bed and saw the dress I wore to my birthday party from the night before. It was crumbled in a ball at the corner of my bed. Directly above it was the infamous blue Post-it Note I wrote Dresden's new number on.

I pulled the dress off my bed and threw it across the room near my hamper. I also plucked the Post-it off my wall and threw it in the garbage. If only everything in life that hurt you was that easy to dispose of. Heartbreak doesn't work that way unfortunately.

I wished it were any other time of year. I would have been fine with Dresden ruining Valentine's Day. But Christmas and New Years were around the corner. That, coupled with my recently bought plane ticket, was nothing more than a painful reminder. A reminder of how Dresden asked me to spend the holidays with him in New York. An offer which was clearly now, null and void.

I mulled around for a few days until Spencer called to check in on me. She had tickets for Cypress Hill and House of Pain at the Santa Monica Civic. Dizzy, Mandie, and Ronnie were going too. Getting high and listening to good music with great friends sounded like fun to me. I took her up on her offer.

Her neighbor, Perry, had an old van from the 70s. And true to 70s form, he had weed. He picked everyone up and we puffed our way out to Santa Monica.

Some of the guys wanted to bring a few joints into the venue. We knew security would search them. They felt Spencer looked more innocent than I did for some reason. Regardless, she shoved a small baggy down her pants and happily strolled through security without a second glance.

The air was thick with marijuana smoke when we strolled into the venue. The guys went to the show floor. I went to the bathroom with Spencer so she could dig the green gold out of her pants. We met up with the guys later by a slowly forming pit. Although we went into the pit together, we lost them shortly after. The pit wasn't as violent as most I was in before. I'm assuming because everyone was high as a kite, including yours truly. The strangers around us formed a wall to keep us from getting hit, and they picked up anyone that fell on the floor. There were no fights. No one was shoving or being a dick. Everyone was in a great mood and into the vibe of the music.

The show went by in a haze, literally. Half of the venue emptied out by the time we found Perry, Mandie, and Ronnie. No one knew where Dizzy was. We walked toward the lobby and found him sleeping on the floor near the back of the venue. The guys picked him up, and we went back to the van.

Dizzy passed out with his head on my lap, while Perry drove us to a nearby Burger King. I would love to say we had a wild night out, but everyone was beat by the time food coma set in. Perry dropped off the guys, and we made our way back to Spencer's.

My night out at Cypress Hill was the highlight of my holidays. I couldn't stop thinking about New York and how I was supposed to be walking the snow-lined streets of Manhattan with Dresden. Instead, I spent most of December sitting alone, watching my plane ticket collect dust on my bedroom dresser.

My hibernation lasted well into 1994. By then, I still hadn't heard from Dresden. I don't know why I expected to. Wanting to break my social coma, I dragged my stitched-up heart to see some friends play a show at the Roxy in Hollywood.

I hadn't gone to the Strip in months, or any club in

Hollywood for that matter. There were many familiar faces at the Roxy, yet I still felt out of place. I assumed it was a mild case of cabin fever from not being out for so long. The reality hit about a half hour later when I walked outside to get some air. I glanced down the empty sidewalks of Sunset Blvd. and knew it was the end of an era.

Grunge music had successfully invaded Los Angeles. Most of the Sunset Strip's glam rock bands packed their things and moved back to their hometowns. Any that remained did a complete image overhaul in the last few months. The days of every guy wanting to have long hair were gone. Long hair wasn't cool anymore. Many chopped off their locks for stylish short dos or radical Mohawks.

The glitzy, sleazy band names were changed to something angry and edgy. The music wasn't fun and light hearted, it was serious and gritty. Hair bands that once packed arenas were dropped like hotcakes by their record labels in exchange for acts like Soundgarden and Pearl Jam.

And makeup? Oh god no. If you were a guy wearing makeup you were made fun of and looked upon like a sad, old relic.

One of the Sunset Strip's landmark clubs, Gazzarri's, closed a few months earlier. Bill Gazzarri, the owner, passed away in early 1991. Although the club remained open for several years after he died, it was never the same. There were hopes and various rumors that someone would revive the club. Despite bands like The Doors and Van Halen gracing it's stage, it was more recently known as a "hair band" club, and no one wanted to invest money in an audience that no longer existed.

Grunge music came in like a tsunami. It annihilated every glam band off the face of the planet and wiped its ass with whoever was left.

The span of my teenage years was spent on the Sunset Strip during its "hair band" era. Now it was over. I was a 20-year-old woman, looking at the skeleton of one of the biggest, ongoing street parties in the country. I grew up in Hollywood during the decade of decadence. It was a time of insanity, gluttony and shamelessness. How the hell was I going to function in a standard social setting? What did normal people do for fun anyway?

I looked at the Roxy marquee. One of the bands was called 'Big Apple' something, and it reminded me I had that unused plane ticket.

My obsession with the city of Manhattan started long before I met Dresden. Despite our falling out or whatever you want to call it, I still wanted to go to New York. I was eager to see The Dakota where John Lennon and Yoko once lived. I wanted to experience a walk through Central Park and stroll through the Lower and Upper East Sides. I wanted to check out the Upper West Side, the backside, front side, and every side that the island of Manhattan had to offer.

I had everything I needed for the trip, except a place to stay. That was quickly taken care of by my old friend, Bam. He recently moved back to Brooklyn and said I could stay with him if I ever made my way out there.

I went back into the Roxy to get a drink. Ronnie tackled me with a hug. We hadn't seen each other since the night of my disastrous birthday party months earlier.

I told Ronnie of my tentative plans to go to New York. He told me I was out of my mind after the way Dresden treated me. I tried to explain I wasn't going for him, but he wasn't buying it. He thought my trip was solely to stalk Dresden. Pixie walked up and overheard our conversation.

"You're going to New York? That's so exciting!

13

When are you going?" she asked.

"I'm not sure when or if I'm going. I have a plane credit I need to use by December, and I've always wanted to go to New York, " I replied.

"If you decide to go, I would totally go with," she said.

I was caught off guard by her interest.

"Are you serious?" I asked.

"I would go in one second. I've always wanted to go there too. We just need to find a place to stay."

"Bam said I could stay with him. Since you know him too, I don't think he would mind both of us crashing. Do you?"

"He totally wouldn't. Oh my god, I'm so excited! We're going to New York!" she squealed.

Pixie grabbed a pen from the bartender and we exchanged phone numbers. We talked about going in the late spring or early summer. But when I came home from the Roxy, I had second thoughts about our tentative travel plans.

Pixie and I had several friends in common from Hollywood, but I didn't know her well. Taking a trip together was a crapshoot. Either our personalities would mesh and we would have the time of our lives, or one of us would live to board the plane back to Los Angeles.

Pixie and I spoke on a regular basis over the next several months. We also talked to Bam and planned our trip for ten days in the middle of August. I had to be over Dresden by then. If not, Pixie could choke me until I was.

I filled her in on my soap opera past with Dresden. I was sick of whining about how he broke my heart. She agreed he handled things badly. She also said it was months ago and to 'get the fuck over it already.' It was a point I couldn't argue with. The latter statement represented Pixie's personality in a nutshell. She didn't tell you what you wanted to hear, she told you what you needed to hear. If you asked her a question, you would get a brutally, honest answer.

While Pixie and I planned our East Coast invasion, I started dating a guitar player named Karl. Karl played for a J-Rock (Japanese Rock) band from Tokyo, called Gravel.

I met Karl at the Whisky through a mutual friend whose band was opening for Gravel one night. He was a bit lanky with light, brown hair and skinny dreads that draped past his shoulders. Pixie and I called him a "Ralph".

A "Ralph" was a term Pixie and I made up based on the character of Ralph Wiggum from The Simpsons. Karl, like Ralph, was nice but a bit cheesy. He had old man humor, which was odd considering he was 21. Listening to him crack jokes was painful. I could hear crickets and tumbleweeds following each of his punch lines.

I wasn't sure what to do about Karl. He was a nice guy and I liked him, but there wasn't a wow factor there. He was like a nicely presented meal that lacked seasoning. Rather than douse Karl in salt, theoretically speaking, I went with the flow for the time being. I was glad my New York trip with Pixie was coming up quickly. It was the perfect opportunity to get away and hopefully come to a decision about Karl before I came back to Los Angeles.

My trip was in the planning stages when I started dating Karl. He wasn't thrilled I was going to New York. I'm not sure what his issue was. I never asked. I didn't care if he had a problem with it. He wasn't my boyfriend. There wasn't a valid reason in my mind for him to be bitching about my trip anyway. The day he put his foot down, I booked my flight with Pixie.

Karl wanted me to call him when I was in New York. That was not on my list of things to do. I wanted complete separation to get my head straight. Not only in regards to him but to get some resolve on my feelings for Dresden. I knew running into him was inevitable. He and Bam were close, but I wasn't going to let that ruin my vacation.

I told Karl I couldn't afford to call him. He said I could call him collect. I said I didn't want him wasting his money and pushed until he relented.

The weeks leading up to our trip flew by. It wasn't long before I found myself rushing through LAX toward a Delta Airlines gate to meet Pixie. I nervously tapped my foot, while we waited to board our red-eye flight.

"What's wrong with you?" Pixie asked.

"I've never flown before." I replied.

"Oh really? That's not a problem, lets have a few cocktails."

"That reminds me, I forgot to bring Lucy's ID with me, damn it!"

"I'll get us drinks here, but call her right now and tell her to Fed Ex her ID to Bam's."

I gave Lucy Bam's address, and the drinking commenced with Pixie. We had a cocktail by our terminal and a few more on the plane until we passed out.

I woke up sometime around 8:00 a.m., as we were landing at JFK airport. We walked outside and almost dropped dead from the scorching temperature and high humidity. It was like walking into a bathroom with the heater on after someone took a hot shower. I never felt anything like it. It was the most horrible weather my thin, California blood encountered.

Pixie and I flagged down a cab as we dripped with sweat. We threw our bags in the trunk and braced ourselves for our ten-day adventure in New York City.

"Where ya going?" the cabby asked.

I smiled and said, "Take us to Brooklyn!"

When we arrived at Bam's in Brooklyn, he was about to walk out the door to go to work.

Bam worked at a legendary record store in Greenwich Village called Bleeker Bob's. The second location was on Melrose in Hollywood, where he and Dresden worked when they lived in L.A. But the Greenwich store had been around since the late '60s.

Bam gave us a spare key and told us to make ourselves at home before leaving. We put our things down and took a look around his spacious, hardwood floor apartment. A small hallway to the left led to a modest kitchen and a small dining table for two. The living room had a fold out sofa bed for Pixie and I, and Bam's bedroom was beyond that, with a window facing the street.

I was beyond excited to be in New York for the first time, but I didn't get much sleep on the red-eye flight. Neither did Pixie. We were too lazy to set up the sofa bed, so we hopped into Bam's bed and took a well-needed slumber.

We woke a few hours later and wanted to take a subway into the city, but we weren't sure how. The only thing Bam mentioned before leaving was that an entrance for the F train was on Church Street, a few blocks away.

I bought a subway map after we landed at JFK. I pulled it out and studied it carefully. It didn't seem complicated. Queens was north, Brooklyn was south, and Manhattan was in between. Pixie and I got dressed and ventured out to find Church Street.

We passed by a few kids playing in the street beside a fire hydrant that was gushing water. Others played stickball. It was something I saw in movies based on New York, but I assumed it was a stereotype. Similar to when people come to Hollywood and think celebrities hang out at Mann's Chinese Theatre or the Hollywood Walk of Fame.

We came upon Church Street and found an entrance for the F train. We walked down a stairway but didn't see a train or train tracks anywhere, just an empty underground walkway that stretched for what seemed like an entire block. We started at each other, wondering what to do when we heard the faint sound of a train. It gradually grew louder until we heard clacking and screeching below our feet. We started screaming and ran back up the stairway.

I looked around and noticed another subway entrance for the F train about a block away. We assumed it was the other end of the walkway we just ran from. After walking down that stairwell, we realized there was an additional set of stairs to descend before reaching the area where the trains stopped. Yes, we were a couple of geniuses.

I looked around the Church St. station and noticed a rat the size of a horse, galloping over bits of trash on the rails below. It was hot and humid. The stench of urine was thick in the air and it hung there like a blanket. Some people stood around, peeking every few seconds into the tunnel to see if the next train was coming. Others were busy popping CDs in and out of their CD players. I hoped the temperature and humidity would taper off once the sun went down. I quickly learned that was my wishful, California way of thinking. The sad reality was it remained hot, humid and miserable during our entire stay, regardless of what time of day it was.

The next train arrived a few minutes later, and we had no trouble navigating our way to Bleeker Bobs. We got our sea legs, or shall I say subway legs rather quickly that afternoon. We were hopping on and off trains, buzzing throughout various boroughs by the end of the day.

Bam had band rehearsal after work the first day we were in town. He wanted us to meet him at a local watering hole called Scrap Bar, when he finished with practice.

Scrap Bar was a tiny, dive bar on MacDougal Street near the West Village in Manhattan. It had a small stairway, maybe about eight or nine steps from the street level that led down to its dark, dingy bar with walls made out of dark, grey boulders. It reminded me of being in a cave. There was a small booth carved into the wall to the left, and a small bar in front of me. Just off to the right was a small phone booth, also inset to the wall.

Last but not least, in the far back were some of the most disgusting bathrooms I ever encountered. They didn't rival those of CBGB's, which I would later find out first hand, but they were still gross nonetheless.

Scrap Bar became our 2$^{nd}$ home on that trip. We quickly befriended its two friendly bartenders, Jesse and Billy, who were also friends of Bam.

Jesse was a thin, rockabilly type with slicked back blond hair, hazel eyes and a slight overbite. Billy, also thin framed, had short, curly dark hair and blue eyes. They set us up with unlimited drinks during our stay; including what would become an East Coast favorite of mine called a Red Devil. And rightly so, because it had every type of hard alcohol you could imagine with the taste of Hawaiian Punch.

Pixie and I went back to Jesse and Billy's apartment that night. It wasn't long before I noticed her and Jesse had a thing for each other. I just wanted to hang out and have a few cocktails, which we did until Billy started making moves on me. I wasn't interested, and him being drunk turned me off even more. I walked him up to the loft where he slept. He passed out before I could pull his blankets over him. When I climbed back down, I noticed Pixie passed out on the living room couch with Jesse. They were happily snuggled up. I didn't want to wake her, so I left.

I walked outside of their apartment building and took a look around. Based on my surroundings, I knew I was somewhere on the upper west side. I had some mild sniffles that morning and my throat was feeling scratchy. The last thing I wanted was to sit on a train, feeling like crap on the long ride back to Brooklyn.

There was a convenience store nearby. I bought a gallon of orange juice and stood on the street corner, taking swigs from the jug like a hobo, as I tried to figure out what to do. The easiest solution was to take a cab, so that's what I did.

When I arrived at Bam's, he was waiting in the living room like an angry father. He asked why Pixie and I didn't come home the night before. He was furious when I told him where we went. And not bringing Pixie home with me made him angrier. Billy and Jesse were not the kind of friends he wanted us spending time with.

Pixie called the apartment shortly after I got back. Bam was in the bathroom, so I answered the phone.

"Marisa?" Pixie asked.

"Yeah, it's me," I whispered. "Dude, I think we're grounded. Bam is pissed we went to Jesse and Billy's last night."

"He's pissed? I'm mad that you left me here!"

Bam came out of the bathroom and asked if I was talking to Pixie. I smiled and handed him the phone. He yelled at Pixie to come home, which she did rather quickly.

When Pixie walked in the door, she sat next to me on the couch and we got an earful from Bam. After he left to work, I got an earful from Pixie about leaving her and to never do it again.

One of the things I liked most about being in New York was the transportation. You didn't need to rent a car to get around the city. The subway system took you everywhere you wanted to go and it was cheap. The train system in Los Angeles at that time was still in its infancy, even now it doesn't compare to New York. Besides, who the hell wants to be underground in a state where earthquakes are commonplace?

I also loved the architecture of New York. Walking around the city by myself and observing the craftsmanship of all the old buildings was breathtaking. I don't mean to bash my hometown, but it was a feeling of history that I rarely felt in Los Angeles. Most buildings in Southern California dated back to the '40s or '50s. I don't know why property owners felt the need to tear down these structures instead of preserve them. There were a few exceptions here and there, but most of the older buildings were located in downtown Los Angeles.

Speaking of old structures, a few nights later Bam's band, the Orphans, were playing a club in the city called Webster Hall. The venue dated back to the late 1800's, and the historical dork in me was chomping at the bit to see it.

When I arrived at Webster Hall with Pixie and Bam, I was overwhelmed by the size of the club. It had four glorious floors with three smaller venues on its different levels, not including its grand ballroom. The ballroom was packed with people and a few go-go dancers, shaking their butts to dance music.

The Orphans were playing in one of the rooms upstairs. When we walked in, Bam introduced us to a few of his female friends, Flo, Dasha, and Jagger. He also introduced us to a go-go dancer named Chrissy, who leaned down from her platform box to give us a warm hug hello. Pixie and I hit it off with the girls and spent the rest of the night cackling and downing cocktails with them.

Shortly after Bam's set, Flo offered to give us a

21

ride home, which we happily accepted. After driving around in circles, she found parking around the corner from Bam's apartment. I told Bam I would help him carry his stuff, so he handed me his snare drum. I ended up lagging behind them, and when I ran to catch up, I tripped over a pothole and fell flat on my face. Bam's snare flew out of my hands, crashed to the ground and rolled down the street until it hit a nearby curb.

All three of them turned around the moment the snare hit the ground. Flo and Pixie started howling and laughing, while Bam yelled that I broke his drum.

I felt bad for dropping Bam's snare, but I couldn't stop laughing at my ridiculous fall. I was laughing so hard I couldn't move. I just lay there in the middle of the residential street, curled up in a ball. It didn't help that Pixie and Flo were caterwauling either. And when Bam yelled at all three of us for making light of the situation, I laughed even more.

I peeled myself off the ground and hobbled over to the girls and Bam. My elbows and knees were cut up pretty bad and he didn't have any Band-Aids. So shortly before bed, I laid down on my back while Pixie wrapped my limbs in toilet paper.

I woke up the next morning looking like a jacked up mummy with pieces of toilet paper all over me. My throat felt a bit scratchy too. I was halfway through my trip, and I wasn't about to let a cold ruin my vacation.

I wanted to venture around the city that afternoon, but I knew it was best that I stay home and try to get well. Pixie went into the city to take some dance classes and Bam left for work, so I had the apartment to myself the entire day. I pulled my sick ass out of bed and hobbled over to a convenience store on Church Street. I bought a small jug of orange juice, a box of green tea and some Alka Seltzer Cold medicine. I came back to Bam's, took a little of all three and slept the entire afternoon.

Pixie came home shortly after the sun went down. Bam followed right after, and to my unfortunate surprise, Dresden was with him.

I hadn't seen or spoken to Dresden in almost a year. Not since the previous November when he ruined my birthday party. I looked like a sick pile of shit and had a cowlick from the nap I just woke from. That wasn't the impression I wanted to make the next time I ran into him.

He and Bam said hello and walked into the kitchen. I quickly ran to the bathroom to take a shower. When I finished, I could hear Bam and Dresden talking in the kitchen. I also heard Pixie yell from the living room that they should make her a drink while they were in there.

I stuck my head out of the bathroom door and looked over into the living room. Pixie looked at me with a raised eyebrow because she knew my history with Dresden.

I was almost done getting ready and hoped Dresden would be gone by the time I finished. Of course he wasn't. But I knew at some point during the trip, I would have to come face to face with him. I couldn't stay in the bathroom the entire night. I took a deep breath and walked into the kitchen.

Bam walked off to the bathroom, leaving Dresden and I alone. I pulled up a chair and sat across from him at Bam's small, kitchen table.

I looked at him for a moment, waiting for him to apologize for the mess he made of my 20th birthday. He knew damn well what I was waiting for. Instead, he quickly broke the silence by asking me if I was having fun in New York, how long I was there for, etc. I thought that after all the crap he put me through, the first thing out of his mouth when he saw me again would be an apology, but no. It was all bullshit small talk, and that's when I realized the kind of person he was.

Dresden was the best person in the world as long as you didn't make waves. But once it wasn't smooth sailing? Bam! He was out of there. He couldn't deal with conflict and didn't care to. If there were a 'Coward' category in the Olympics, he would've brought home the gold every time.

I wasn't expecting him to roll out the red carpet or give me a lengthy mea culpa. I just wanted him to take responsibility over what happened on my birthday. To just say a simple, "I'm sorry." But as I listened to him chatter about a whole lot of nothing, I knew he was never going to apologize.

I could've pushed the issue and called him out on ruining my birthday, among other things, but I didn't want to start the night on a bad note. I also knew it was pointless. No matter how hard you try, you can't change a person. Can you make them better? Yes. But you can't change them. I had to accept Dresden for the person he was.

Now don't get me wrong, despite all my bellyaching I didn't hate Dresden or think he was the worst person on earth. It's not like he killed a member of my family. We all have our personality quirks, and I knew deep down he had a good heart. This would be one of those things we would never see eye to eye on. Rather than fight a losing battle, I just let it go. I let go of the hurt, the disappointment, and most importantly, the love I had for him.

I put a smile on my face and pretended like nothing bad happened. I told him about a few adventures with Pixie while being in New York and how excited I was to be there. Bam walked in and unintentionally broke up the conversation by talking about band details with Dresden. I took that as my cue to exit and joined Pixie in the living room.

When Pixie finished getting ready, Dresden dropped us off at a club called the Limelight. The Limelight was an old neo-gothic, brownstone building. It served as a church dating back to the mid 1800's until it was bought and converted to a club in the early 1980s. It had a large dance floor with dancers in cages dancing above you. The enormous stained glass windows scaled the length of its walls and the upper balconies gave you a widespread view of the narrow, semi-Goth club below. It was my favorite of all the clubs I went to while being in New York.

After a few cocktails at the Limelight, the three of us hopped on a train and made our way back to Bam's in Brooklyn.

I was feeling a bit shook up over seeing Dresden earlier. Bam sensed that and started wrestling with me to take my mind off of things. He grabbed me in the hallway and put me into a headlock. My face was near his ass as I tried to wiggle myself out of the chokehold. That's when he let out a thunderous, roaring fart right in my face.

"Eww!" I yelled.

He let go of the chokehold. I ran away like a squealing piglet over to Pixie, who was laughing as I hopped into our sofa bed.

"Oh yeah? You think that's funny?" he asked Pixie.

He ran over to us, jumped on the sofa bed and gave her a hard slap right on her thigh, by her ass. She let out a big yelp, but the three of us started laughing when we saw the red handprint left behind.

The remaining days in New York were a blur. It was a standard routine of visiting Bam at Bleeker Bob's, then heading to the Scrap Bar in the evenings or other bars like Niagra and Continental. We did a few touristy things like see the Statue of Liberty and the World Trade Center. We took a long walk through Central

Park and passed a man and his kids digging change out of one of its glorious fountains. And of course being the psycho Beatle fan I am, I had to see The Dakota where John and Yoko lived. I also went to Strawberry Fields, the memorial park in Central Park dedicated to John Lennon.

Even with all the landmarks we visited, I still didn't get to see everything I wanted. However, Pixie was staying in New York for a few more weeks, simply because she wanted to. But such is the life of a rich girl. Being able to change plans on a whim without any financial stress whatsoever, whereas I had run out of vacation days at my crappy job and had to get back to Los Angeles.

With my last few days in New York coming to a close, I knew I had to end things with Karl when I came home. I think I knew that before I left. I hoped that being away from him would make me miss him, but it backfired. My trip made me realize how much I enjoyed being single.

When I came back to Los Angeles, I told Karl it wasn't working between us. I felt bad. He took the news well, although he thought I hooked up with Dresden and blamed him for our breakup.

Shortly after Karl and I broke up, I happily rebounded back to the single life. I recently turned 21 and was back in touch with my old friend, Eric, who I knew from the Blackboard Jungle days. He had just started a gig as a DJ at a new afterhours club in Hollywood called Seven Seas.

Seven Seas was part of a semi- abandoned, three story building on Hollywood Blvd. near La Brea Ave, but the club only occupied the first level. Back in its heyday, Seven Seas served as an island-themed nightclub during World War II. It was later transformed into a supper club in the 1960s. The building sat across from Mann's Chinese Theatre and could only be accessed through an entrance in the parking lot.

Seven Seas was run similar to the previous afterhours, The Church, which was a semi-modern day speakeasy. All revenue generated by the club was considered 'donations'.

Admission to Seven Seas was free, but they recommended a 'donation' at the door. There was a makeshift bar with no cost for drinks, but again, it was casually mentioned that you make a 'donation' of $5 per drink. You were never forced to 'donate' anything, but everyone was well aware of how things worked.

During the first couple of weeks, attendance was sparse. There weren't more than thirty people at any given time. But a month later, word got around about Seven Seas.

Spencer and I used to stroll right in using Eric's clout and dance around the main floor to our heart's content. That soon changed, and Eric had to start putting us on his guest list. We also had to confine ourselves to Eric's DJ booth. It was the only area at Seven Seas with a little bit of wiggle room among the packed floor.

Most of the people who went to Seven Seas were the old Sunset Strip crowd. People like Mandie and Dizzy from the Glamour Punks and a few of the guys from Blackboard Jungle. I still saw those guys from time to time, but it wasn't every weekend like it used to be until Seven Seas opened.

Many of us found ourselves a bit displaced when the hair band scene took a nosedive. Back in the day, you could stroll up to the Sunset Strip or go to a show and see all your friends there. Sure, people went to shows here and there, but it wasn't the same. There wasn't a music scene in Los Angeles. I knew Seven Seas could never recreate that, but it was nice to have a watering hole where I could meet up with my old friends on a Saturday night.

Seven Seas was a fraction of the entertainment that Spencer and I partook in every weekend during that time. Our evenings usually started around 11:00 p.m. when I would pick her up and go to the Whisky. We knew the manager and some of the bouncers there, so we would hang out with them and have cocktails after the club closed.

Being at the Whisky after closing time was so much fun with those guys. It was like having our own personal jungle gym. One of the bouncers was a prankster and always did crazy stunts. We nicknamed him 'Luby' one night after he snorted a lubricated condom through his nose and coughed it out.

Spencer and I would hang out at the Whisky with the guys until 2:30 or 3:00 in the morning. Then we would go to the Del Taco on Highland and Santa Monica where we loaded up on chicken soft tacos. We'd take our bountiful meal over to Seven Seas and sit in the parking lot, indulging in our tasty treats until Seven Seas opened around 3:00 a.m. or so.

Eric played a mix of songs from dance music to things like Rage Against the Machine and Nine Inch Nails. Spencer and I would dance the entire night, working off those chicken tacos. The final song of the night was usually "Jailhouse Rock". Spencer and I were exhausted by then but we always loved that song. We would join hands and swing dance while our sweaty hair popped out of our floppy, once pristine ponytails.

But as the old saying goes, "all good things must come to an end", and that's exactly what happened to Seven Seas when it was raided a short time later. The guys who ran the club laid low for a few months and reopened it some time later, but it wasn't the same. Seven Seas had run its course and it wasn't long before it was shut down for its final time. The property sits next door to where the *Jimmy Kimmel Live* show is now filmed. I believe it has since been remodeled and taken over by a few retail businesses.

Shortly after ringing in the New Year of 1995, rumors were floating around among the old school crowd that Dizzy wasn't doing so well.

The last time I saw Dizzy was at Seven Seas. A short time later, he moved to Las Vegas and it was no secret that he had a problem with alcohol. Before he went to Vegas, he began having seizures as a result of his drinking.

I spoke with Dizzy a handful of times after he moved. I lost touch with him a shortly after. I tried to be positive and hoped he was getting the help that he so desperately needed. So you can imagine my surprise when Spencer broke the news about Dizzy's passing shortly after Valentine's Day. He was only 23.

The services were held in Las Vegas. I was angry that I couldn't afford to make the road trip with Spencer. Luckily, a benefit show was thrown in memory of Dizzy at the Coconut Teaszer, exactly one month after he passed away.

On the roster to perform at the Teaszer were bands like God Zoo, The Things (formerly Swingin Thing), and the Fizzy Bangers. The final band included Alley from God Zoo on bass, Brian Waters of the Fizzy Bangers on guitar, and Mandie from the Glamour Punks on vocals. They even brought out Punk Rock Dave, the unofficial band mascot of the Glamour Punks. I believe someone from a band called Press Darlings was playing 2$^{nd}$ guitar, and I can't recall who was playing drums, unfortunately. Collectively, it was a one off jam session and they called themselves Damage Inc.

They played Glamour Punks favorites like "Video Nasty", "Roach Motel", and "Woman". My ex from The Kids, Sebastian, went onstage to sing backup on one of the songs. Brent Muscat from Faster

Pussycat was there too, along with many old school Hollywood kids I hadn't seen in years.

Pixie, Faye, and Spencer were also there. The Glamour Punks had been broken up for a few years at that point, but it felt like old times being in the front row, rocking out like we used to when we were teenage schoolgirls.

Shortly after Dizzy's passing, I befriended a bassist named Randall. He frequented the same crowd I did, so he knew people like Pixie, Spencer, and Mandie. We would all go record shopping and see movies together. He was also with me when I made the crazy decision to get my tongue pierced.

I went back and forth with the idea for months. I wasn't serious about it until Randall and I went shopping on Melrose, and I passed by a piercing shop. I figured I would ask about the procedure and hope that whatever they told me would scare me out of doing it.

I think the cost was about $30-40. They mentioned there would be some swelling for the first few days, but sucking on ice or non-dairy popsicles could relieve that. They also mentioned I would need to rinse with an antiseptic like Listerine after every meal and beverage aside from water.

It didn't sound bad, but I was still a bit scared. Randall suggested I think about it while we shopped, and if I wasn't ready to do it by the time we were ready to leave we could forget about it and go home.

We continued shopping and the things the piercer said earlier didn't seem to bother me. I told Randall I wanted to go through with it and we walked back to the piercing shop.

After signing some paperwork they took me behind a large shoji screen, which separated a tattoo chair from the rest of the shop. It was a tiny area only big enough to fit the chair, my piercer and me. Pat, my piercer, was a tall, buff, bald guy with cork gauges in each of his earlobes and covered in tattoos.

I sat on the tattoo chair and Pat had me rinse with Listerine. He slapped on a pair of plastic gloves and used a pair of tongs to pull my tongue out so he could get a good look at where to pierce me. He lifted my tongue up and down with the tongs, marked an area and lifted my tongue up and down again to confirm he had the right spot. He grabbed a hollow needle and told me to take three deep breaths. He was going to pierce me on the third breath.

I breathed once.

I breathed twice.

On the third breath, I felt pain that could only be compared to the throbbing of when you accidentally bite down on your tongue.

The pain was gone within seconds. I was about to stand up, but I started feeling nauseous.

Pat took off his gloves and asked, "Hey honey, are you okay?"

"It got really hot in here all of a sudden, I feel kind of dizzy. You look a bit fuzzy too," I replied.

"You're probably going into a light state of shock. Just lay back and take deep breaths," he said, rubbing my hand.

"Hey what's going on back there? Did you barf yet?" Randall asked from the other side of the shoji screen.

"Would you shut up? I don't feel good," I said, wearily.

I lay back in the chair and Pat put both of my hands on my stomach like he was arranging a corpse in a coffin. He told me to breath with him as he took deep breaths in and out. I was so embarrassed. I was breathing like I was going into labor, but Pat was a good sport about it. He sat there breathing with me for a couple of minutes then left to get me a glass of water.

31

My tongue healed quickly. A few weeks later, I went back to get my bellybutton pierced. I had been through the worst with my tongue; so I thought getting my belly button done would be a breeze. Being the big chicken I am, I went into shock again and Pat resumed his breathing exercises to keep me from passing out.

When Randall and I started hanging out it was usually with other friends in a platonic setting. But over time, that changed and it became us two. Then the inevitable happened, we made out one night. On another night, it went a step further, and I literally woke one morning to find I was in a full-blown relationship with Randall.

I genuinely liked being with Randall. He was a lot of fun to be around. But I hadn't dated anyone since Karl, and I wasn't sure I wanted to be in a relationship with Randall for various reasons.

For one, I was enjoying my freedom. Not that I was out sleeping around. I was just enjoying my alone time and didn't want anyone to answer to.

Another issue was his recent break up of a seven-year relationship with his ex-girlfriend, Lindsey.

Lindsey was his grade school sweetheart, his first girlfriend, his first love, the girl he lost his virginity to, etc. Her list of credentials was enough to build a pedestal, which Randall put her on. I couldn't have been a bigger rebound unless I had a trampoline strapped to my ass.

When I started dating Randall, he was still hanging out with Lindsey sporadically, but "just as friends", so he said. He would go to her parent's house to watch new episodes of their favorite shows. They would go record shopping, she'd bring him lunch at work, and he even went to her dad's wedding.

Lindsey also went to all of Randall's shows. She was a sweet girl, so it was hard for me to be a bitch to her over the time she was spending with Randall. But right when I was at the peak of being fed up with the situation, she began dating a co-worker of hers named Dale.

I assumed having Dale in her life would make her time with Randall dwindle down considerably, but it didn't. The time she spent with Randall was almost equal to the time he spent with me. I can't fathom what was going through Dale's mind with all this. I can't imagine he would've been okay with it.

It was around the same time that my 2$^{nd}$ trip to New York with Pixie was coming up. I welcomed a break from the Randall and Lindsey soap opera, but I was also on edge. I knew with me being gone, he would have free reign over his time with Lindsey, since I wouldn't be there to bitch about it in person.

A few things had changed since the last time Pixie and I were in New York. For one, the Scrap Bar was gone. We also wouldn't be staying with Bam. We were staying with his friend, Jagger, a door girl from Scrap Bar who we befriended on our last trip.

I would be flying solo to New York because Pixie was going to Boston a few days early to visit some friends. She planned on taking the Amtrak into New York on the day I landed.

After arriving at La Guardia airport, I was still weary from my red-eye flight. I gathered my things and walked outside to hail a cab. A man claiming to a limo driver approached me.

"Hi Miss, where are you off to today?" he asked.

"Lower Manhattan, why?" I asked, cautiously.

"Wonderful, so is she," he replied, pointing to an elderly woman in a nearby limo.

"Oh, that's nice," I said, casually.

"Would you like to join her? If you split the cost of the limo with her, it would be about the same as you taking a cab by yourself."

"No offense, but I don't know you. You could

be some kind of crazy rapist or something," I said, bluntly.

"I can assure you I'm not," he said laughing. "If you'd like to speak with her, she can vouch for me. It's a good deal, only $50 out of your pocket."

I walked over to the limo and the elderly woman peeked her head out, smiled and introduced herself as Amelia.

"Nice to meet you Amelia. What's the deal with this guy?" I asked.

"He's fine. This is the third time I've used this driver. He runs a family business and is just trying to make some extra money by adding an additional passenger," she said, smiling.

"Alright, you've got yourself a passenger Jeeves. But don't pull any crap. I may be small, but I'm a Latina with a bad temper," I said, raising an eyebrow.

Amelia and I talked about where we grew up on the ride into the city. I was surprised to find not only was she from Southern California but also grew in up in my hometown of Rosemead. We spoke about various shops and defunct businesses I remembered vividly as a kid.

I was dropped off first at Jagger's. Amelia gave me a gentle hug goodbye before I climbed out of the limo. The driver took my bags out, accepted my $50 in cash and drove off.

I stood on the sidewalk in front of Jagger's apartment building and looked at my bags. One was missing, a small duffel bag that contained my shoes and undergarments.

I knew I didn't leave it in the trunk of the limo. I watched the driver pull the bags out. Amelia had one bright, red suitcase that stood out among my black luggage. I retraced my steps and remembered where I left it. My bags were on the ground beside me when the limo driver approached me, except for that small duffel bag, which was sitting on a bench next to me.

The only shoes I had were the black and white Converse on my feet. I could make the sneakers work with some of my outfits, but shopping for new undergarments wasn't in my budget. It's not like I had a choice, I couldn't go commando during my entire trip. I knew Jagger could recommend some cheap stores in the city, so I picked up my things and made my way into the apartment building.

Jagger lived with her mom, Elisa, near CBGB's in lower Manhattan. They had a spare bedroom in their apartment where Pixie and I would be staying. Elisa and Jagger were outspoken, Italian women with Brooklyn accents. Jagger had a bit more tact than her mother, but I found Elisa's boldness refreshing, not to mention funny.

Shortly after unloading my luggage, I called the airport's lost and found, but no one had turned in my bag yet. After giving them Jagger's info, we ventured around the hot and humid streets of New York in search of affordable skivvies for yours truly.

Pixie arrived after we returned from shopping. Jagger mentioned she had a boyfriend in Staten Island who she would be visiting off and on during our stay. She left once Pixie arrived, but gave us a spare key and said she would be home later that evening.

When Jagger left, Elisa told us she was going to a family wedding in Long Island that afternoon. She wanted us to help her get ready.

Personally, I'm a man trapped in a woman's body. I can't accessorize to save my life. Hell, I can barely put on a decent face of makeup and pick out an outfit for myself, much less a stranger. But Pixie was a girly girl. She was more than happy to take up my slack, while I sat on the couch and watched TV.

Elisa had a dress picked out. She only wanted her hair and makeup done. The dress was laid out beside me on the couch. It was the gaudiest thing I ever saw. It was a long, sequined dress in a bright shade of seaweed green. But no one was asking for my opinion, so I kept that critique to myself.

After Pixie did Elisa's hair and makeup it was time for her to put on the dress. She grabbed that awful seaweed wrap and went to the bathroom. When she came out, she asked Pixie to zip her up. There was almost a 1-inch gap between each side of the zipper tracks. I didn't know how Pixie was going to get her in that thing.

Pixie repeatedly told her to suck in her gut, but the zipper wouldn't go up. Out of nowhere, Elisa complained that her dog needed to go to the bathroom. Her pets weren't my responsibility, but she was letting us stay there for free. It was the least I could do. I also felt uncomfortable watching Pixie try to stuff her in that dress, so I took the elderly German Shepard for a stroll.

I came back about five minutes later and Pixie was still trying to get Elisa into that dress. I offered my help. Pixie and I were giggling over this almost impossible feat when Elisa told us to go fuck a horse. Pixie and I burst out laughing.

Elisa didn't want to change outfits. We had to make that dress work, even if it meant using a stick of butter and a shoehorn to get her into that thing.

I don't know how we made that fabric stretch but we did and finally got the dress to zip up. She was packed tighter than a can of tuna. I wouldn't have been surprised if she cracked a rib while trying to get into a car.

After Elisa wiggled off to the wedding, Pixie and I had the place to ourselves. We worked up an appetite getting Elisa into that dress, so we wandered around the neighborhood and brought back a large pizza.

Jagger came home a few hours later. She told us

about a club called Coney Island High. Coney opened a few months earlier and according to Jagger, it picked up where Scrap Bar left off. It was the new watering hole for our New York friends.

Coney Island High was a three level club owned by Jesse Malin from the legendary punk band, D Generation. It was located on the historical St. Marks Place in the East Village, which was a small street that stretched about three blocks and had become the heart of the city's counter culture.

The venues on St. Marks dated back to the '60s, hosting celebrities like Andy Warhol, Jimi Hendrix and Abbie Hoffman. Even Jeff Buckley had a residency at a club on St. Marks. The street also hosted graffiti artists from the '80s like Keith Haring and Basquiat.

The first time I saw the outside of Coney Island High, it reminded me of an entrance to a whimsical circus ride. The sign was painted fire engine red with the words, "Coney Island High" written in yellow. Black stars separated each word and the sign stretched across the wide entrance, which had several doors that were also painted red. Each door bore the face of a character similar to Alfred E. Neuman, the fictitious mascot and cover boy of *Mad Magazine*.

While the outside of Coney Island High and its main bar area rings sharp in my mind, my memory is foggy when it comes to the other levels inside the club. So bear with me, it's only been about 20 years since I've been in that establishment.

Upon entering the main, front door there was a stairway along the left side of the wall that led you up to the main bar area. The walls were the same bright shade of red, as were the few booths that lined one side of the wall. Opposite the booths was the main bar with strange artwork hanging behind on its wall.

If I'm not mistaken there was a basement. I can't remember if it had a small bar. I went down there once with Pixie, but I was under the influence of numerous Red Devils.

Lastly, the main level of the club had a small stage where bands played. The club hosted their own version of *The Dating Game* on our first night there. The host was in need of bachelorettes, so he approached Pixie and Chrissy while I was in the restroom. They both initially told him no, but when he offered them free drinks for the night, they quickly agreed. After getting them fresh cocktails, they walked onstage and sat on high-top stools next to another bachelorette.

Pixie and Chrissy had no interest in the bachelor. They purposely gave ridiculous answers so they wouldn't get picked, and it worked like a charm. Once the bachelor chose the other bachelorette, Pixie, Chrissy and I made our way back upstairs to the main bar. By that time, regulars like Dresden, Bam, Billy, and Frankie had arrived. Everyone crammed into one of Coney's red booths. I sat between Bam and Frankie.

Frankie and I met toward the later part of the Sunset Strip days. He stayed with Bam and Dresden in the Melrose house during the brief time he lived in L.A. Frankie was easy on the eyes with long, light brown hair to his shoulders and bright green eyes. He was fun to flirt with, but it never went past that because of my relationship with Randall. It was a rocky relationship, but a relationship nonetheless. Now, if I were single at that time…no of course I wouldn't have slept up with Frankie. He was a friend of Dresden's and that was too close for comfort. But I wouldn't have turned down a make out session.

I was leaning over the table, talking to Pixie when a girl walked up and punched Frankie in the side of his head. She followed her right hook by throwing her drink in his face and stormed off.

Frankie was resting his arm along the top of the booth behind me. I'm guessing from afar it looked like he had his arm around me. Without missing a beat, Frankie grabbed his drink with one hand and a napkin in the other.

"Are you okay?" I asked.

He wiped his face and said, "Yeah, I'm fine."

"Was that your girlfriend or something?"

"No, that definitely wasn't my girlfriend."

"That crazy bitch? HELL NO she ain't his girlfriend. She wishes," Dresden added.

"Let me guess, that was a girl you hooked up with?" I asked.

"Exactly," Frankie confirmed.

The *Fatal Attraction* moment was quickly forgotten and we ordered a round of drinks, which included my East Coast favorite, the Red Devil.

Pixie and I spent almost every night at Coney Island High during that trip. But this time around, keeping up my cheery demeanor around Dresden wasn't difficult like the last time I was in New York. A year had passed and wounds were healed. I was finally able to see him for the fun person he was when we first met. I'll admit it did tug at my heartstrings a little when I saw Dresden on that trip. But I think it was more novelty of what was once our love affair. Or shall I say what I THOUGHT was love. I couldn't imagine going through that emotional rollercoaster all over again.

The remaining days in New York were spent bouncing around different bars like Niagra, Continental, and of course, Coney Island High. It was a ten-day blur of drinking, mixed in with nonstop hijinks and one strange encounter that I can only compare as having a *Godfather* moment.

It was about four or five in the morning. I had just walked out of Coney Island High with Pixie after a long night of cocktails and cackling with our friends when she mentioned she was hungry. I jumped on the gluttonous bandwagon and said I wouldn't mind a bite either. We ran into Bam's friend, Dasha, on the way out and told her we were starving. She said to meet us out front in a few minutes and she would take us somewhere to eat.

The scene on St. Marks was different from when we arrived a few hours earlier. The small street was usually a mix of tourists and locals during normal hours. Now it was a mix of locals and tourists that had transformed into belligerent drunks, except for one, unfortunate guy we spotted across the street from Coney.

The poor fellow had passed out while sitting on an apartment stoop. His head was resting on one arm, which lay across his knees. The other arm hung alongside his legs with his hand dangling off a step. In front of him was a mountain of pink barf.

Pixie and I were worried he might get mugged. We yelled a few things to wake him up, but he was in a perfect state of slumber. Not wanting to go near him or his vomit, we took a few pictures of him to commemorate the moment and continued talking amongst ourselves.

Dasha came outside and mentioned a pizza place around the corner she could take us to. Next door to the pizza place was a bar she wanted to go to first. It was owned by someone she called "Uncle Sal".

We walked into the bar and it was more like a dimly lit lounge. It wasn't crowded like Coney Island High, and we were the only young riff raff in there. The rest of the clientele consisted of about ten to fifteen older gentlemen. They were all dressed in suits, scattered about the lounge, sipping on their drinks.

I was a little tipsy at that point and felt uncomfortable, so I ordered a Shirley Temple. Two older gentlemen approached us and Dasha gave the introductions. Pixie reiterated she was hungry, and one of the men told her he would take her next door to get food.

I didn't want her to go with that guy, but there was no subtle way to tell her in front of them. Thinking with her stomach as always, she walked off with one of the older gentleman to get pizza.

Dasha pointed to a booth in a corner where a few other gentlemen were sitting around chatting and smoking cigars. She asked if I wanted to join her. I told her I was going to sit at the bar because cigar smoke bothered me. She left me to sip on my Shirley Temple and joined the gentlemen.

I spoke with the bartender for almost an hour. I was concerned about Pixie's whereabouts, especially since she was supposed to be next-door. I was about to get up and go next door when Pixie walked in. She was carrying a large pizza box with both hands and had a slice of pizza hanging out of her mouth. She pulled out a stool next to me and placed her pizza box on the counter.

"Where the hell have you been? I've been freaking out for the last hour," I whispered.

"We were just next door, why? What's the problem?"

"You were gone a long time just to pick up a pizza."

"The place was actually closed when we got there, but they opened it right up for us. They made the pizza I wanted and gave it to me for free," she said, smiling.

Pixie ordered a glass of red wine and that's when the reality hit me. Again, it could've been my paranoia looking for things that weren't there, but I couldn't shake that uncomfortable feeling. It was a bad feeling I had the moment we walked into that place. I was also exhausted and felt it was best that we get out of there.

I abruptly told Pixie I was tired and wanted to leave. She said she was tired too. We walked over to

Dasha and told her we were leaving. She wanted to stay. Pixie and I thanked her and everyone at the table for their kind hospitality and promptly left the lounge.

The sun was beginning to rise as we strolled down St. Marks, and the unfortunate drunk across from Coney Island High was still in the same spot. Only now, he was lying across a step, curled up in the fetal position and with a bigger pile of barf in front of him.

When we passed CBGBs, I noticed Pixie sipping on a glass of wine. She drank freely like we were strolling down the streets of Las Vegas where drinking on a public street was legal.

"You stole that glass from the bar?" I asked.

"I didn't steal it. I just wasn't finished with my drink yet," she said, casually.

Our last day in New York consisted of a food run on steroids. We went all over the island of Manhattan, as well as a few boroughs. Pixie became a fan of New York cuisine not available in Los Angeles, so she brought a piece of it back with her, or pieces I should say.

We stopped at the sandwich shop in Brooklyn next to Bam's old apartment to get a few subs. Then we went to a bakery a friend of hers recommended that had the best cannolis in the city. And last but not least, the venue we frequented most during both of our New York trips, our beloved Joe's Pizza near Washington Square Park.

Joe's Pizza not only fed our empty bellies on many a drunken night, but it was also our northern star. It became our point of reference anytime we were lost in the city. If we stood in front of Joe's Pizza, we knew what direction was home.

Pixie ordered a large pizza and told the staff she was taking it back to Los Angeles. They were so flattered by her dedication that they individually wrapped each slice and packaged them in butcher paper for her.

After coming back to Jagger's, I got a call from La Guardia airport. Someone turned in my missing bag, and I could pick it up when I checked in for my flight.

Leaving New York was bittersweet for me. I fell in love with the city and the punk rock scene on St. Marks that was very much alive. It was where people went out in droves and supported the music. It didn't compare to the snore fest in L.A.

Looking back on it now, I wish I made more of an effort to explore St. Marks while I was there. I didn't return to New York for several years. And when I did, it was a completely different place. Many of the independent storefronts on St. Marks had disappeared and gotten a facelift to accommodate franchises like Pinkberry and Chipotle. Even Coney Island High was torn down to make way for condos. Yes condos! This was the place that once housed punk bands like Murphy's Law and where Joey Ramone held his annual birthday bash. Pixie and I actually met Johnny Ramone there during that last trip. To have a musical landmark and all those old vintage storefronts torn down for snooty condos and chain stores seemed like historical blasphemy.

Shortly after Pixie and I arrived at La Guardia airport, I got my bag back. As I went through my things, I thought about the Randall and Lindsey situation waiting for me in L.A.

Aside from the time Randall and Lindsey were spending together, another issue was the collage of pictures hanging on Randall's bedroom wall. We had dated for months and were exclusive. I was livid that he kept that shrine up, especially when there was not ONE picture of us anywhere in his bedroom.

"It's not a shrine, its just pictures and they've been there forever. I forgot they were there," he said.

"Yeah right. And I don't like that you are spending as much time with her as you spend with me. There's a reason they call it 'breaking up'. That being that you actually BREAK UP," I said.

"You can't expect me to cut her out of my life because we aren't dating. We've known each other for a long time."

"I didn't say cut her out of your life. If you want to chat once in a while that's fine. But it's not right for you to hang out with her every week, especially at her house."

We argued back and forth. He assured me nothing was going on. He didn't want to end things with me and promised he would cut back on his time with Lindsey.

I was close to breaking up with him, but I felt bad. The entire situation was a pain in my ass. I didn't want to deal with any of it, but I said I would be patient. Well, that lasted all of about a week.

Randall got on the guest list to see a band called Material Issue and told me he was taking Lindsey. He made that decision before asking me if I wanted to go. His defense in giving her priority was that it was one of her favorite bands, whereas they were not one of mine.

Naturally, I flipped out and we got into a huge fight. I couldn't comprehend how he thought this was normal behavior for two exes. He couldn't understand why I was making a big deal over what he thought to be nothing.

I was tired of fighting over Lindsey. It was a pointless argument. Knowing our relationship had run its course; I used the fight and Lindsey as an excuse to break up with Randall.

I knew I should've called it quits from the beginning, but I always try to give people the benefit of the doubt. The obvious assumption would be to say he was cheating on me the entire time. But to this day, I don't have concrete evidence either way.

I thought he and Lindsey would get back together after we broke up. Strangely they didn't. She married Dale a few years later, and they're still together to this day.

*WALKING CONTRADICTION*

# 2

# IT ALWAYS COMES IN THREES

*I* was fresh off of my second trip to New York when I received news that my dad's wife, Pamela, passed away. I knew she struggled with several health issues throughout her life, but I was still surprised.

I know I'm horrible for saying this, but something positive did come as the result of her passing. That being, I got my dad back.

During the years he was with Pamela, we didn't see much of each other. He was wrapped up in his relationship with her and her three sons. They went on family vacations that I no longer took with my dad. Naturally, I was jealous. Her kids had become closer to my own dad than I was. But I was thrown off guard by their actions after her funeral.

They went to live with their biological father in

Oregon, which was understandable. But they stopped all contact with my dad after Pamela died. I found that so disrespectful, considering he always treated them like his own kids.

Maybe my dad and I getting close again was only because he didn't have Pamela. Perhaps it would've happened eventually, who knows. I didn't care either way. I was glad to have him back in my life on a regular basis and wanted to catch up on the time we lost. That's when he broke the news that he had developed throat cancer.

My dad was a smoker for most of his life. He quit a few years earlier, but apparently, it wasn't soon enough. He was about to start a round of chemotherapy and radiation, which he played off like it was nothing. I knew it was. Going through one of those treatments was drastic. The combination of both made it clear he was battling a vigorous form of cancer. He talked down the situation and joked about carrying the chemo bag around his waist in a "fanny pack". I wanted to have a meltdown, but I knew it wouldn't do any good. My dad would never admit to how bad it was anyway. He wanted to keep the cancer talk light, so I didn't press the issue and tried to remain positive for his sake.

Shortly after reconnecting with my dad, Pixie and I spoke with Spencer about what to do for New Years. I had never gone to Las Vegas before. That was all they needed to hear. We planned on going with another girlfriend of ours, and unfortunately, Randall.

Randall and I were only weeks out of our breakup. He was the last person I wanted to be around. To this day, a disagreement remains between the girls and myself on why they invited him in the first place.

My stance was they invited Randall without any regard for my feelings. Mainly because they were friends with him before we were started dating.

The girls claim I was so private with my relationships that I never told them we broke up. Had they known, they wouldn't have invited him. Either way, Randall ended up going. But regardless of his presence, I had a great time ringing in 1996.

A few months into the New Year, I finally got a break from Randall. We had numerous friends in common, so it was hard to get away from him. I needed space to get over any bad feelings I had toward him. I eventually did, and when we saw each other out and about, things were fine between us. We got along great and strangely, everything went back to the way it was when we were platonic friends. I guess it never should've been more than that to begin with.

One such night was at the Coconut Teaszer. A bunch of us went to see Gilby Clarke perform who was doing solo shows outside of Guns N' Roses.

His opening act was a band from Phoenix, Arizona called the Beat Angels. Randall and I became instant fans. The best way I could describe their music would be a mix of '60s rock like the Rolling Stones with a touch of the Clash. Coincidentally, one of the guitar players, Keith, was almost the spitting image of Joe Strummer from the Clash, except about 4 inches taller.

Keith was originally from Detroit and stood about 6'4", which included his rockabilly styled pompadour. Randall and I got a chance to talk with him and some of the other guys in the Beat Angels after the show. They were down-to-earth guys, and I took an unexpected liking to Keith.

Keith and I kept in touch after that night. As the months passed, the Beat Angels dipped in and out of Los Angeles for shows. And every time they came to town, I would hang out with Keith.

While Keith was away living in Phoenix, we kept in touch through phone calls and the wondrous new invention of email! My dad recently bought me my first home computer as a birthday gift. I was excited to be a part of the information highway! I had also just bought my first cell phone and pager. A dirty pay phone was no longer my only option to make public calls. I was able to call people back from the comfort of my clean, analog cell phone, which was the size of a small baguette.

I know this sounds pathetic, but dating Keith was the only good thing going on in my life at the time. Aside from being miserable at work, I was having serious anxiety over my dad's battle with cancer. Miraculously, he hadn't lost his hair yet. Aside from being a little more fatigued than usual, he was considerably active and in good spirits.

After a particularly bad day at work, I was on the verge of a serious meltdown. I needed to get out of Los Angeles, even if it was just for a day. I came home to an empty house and called Keith on the verge of tears. He told me to drop my things and hop on a flight to Phoenix to visit him.

I had a computer, but my modem connection was slower than pouring molasses. I wanted to be out of the house before my mom or sisters came home. I hung up with Keith, hopped off my computer and immediately called Southwest Airlines.

Southwest had one ticket left on a flight that departed in three hours. The rest of the evening flights to Phoenix were sold out. I didn't have a credit card, so I couldn't buy the ticket over the phone. My only option was to buy it in person with cash or a check. But if someone called with a credit card or showed up in person to buy the seat before I got there, I was screwed. I threw a few things in a duffel bag and within five minutes I was running out my front door.

I raced to the Burbank Airport and hit a wall of traffic on the I-5 freeway, which added to the mountain of anxiety I already had.

When I made it to the Southwest counter, I was grateful to find that the ticket was still available. I wrote a check for my ticket as the plane started to board.

I spent two days decompressing in Phoenix with Keith and poured out my fears over my dad's health. He mentioned his drummer was battling and losing his fight with cancer, which made me feel worse.

Keith took me to breakfast on my last day in Phoenix. We said we loved each other, which we had been saying for weeks. Strangely though, our relationship status was something we never spoke about. I had no desire to be with anyone else. He wasn't seeing anyone that I knew of, although he did speak with his ex-girlfriend and ex-wife from time to time. But that was the kind of person he was, and it didn't bother me. He was a sweet, friendly guy. I couldn't imagine him having a scorned ex or anyone saying a bad word about him.

We weren't geographically desirable, so I wasn't sure if a monogamous relationship was something I should ask for. I had never been in a long distance relationship before. I didn't know what the rules were.

To make matters more confusing, he made plans to go back to Detroit for New Years when I assumed we would be spending it together. Adding that to our questionable relationship status, I felt like I was leaving Phoenix with more anxiety than when I arrived, and rightly so. A few weeks later, he dropped the bomb that he was getting back together with his ex-girlfriend.

I put my heartbreak on the backburner to make New Year's plans with Pixie and Spencer. After having such a blast in Vegas the previous year, the girls wanted to do it again. Generally speaking, it seemed like a good idea. But as the days grew closer to the trip, I became less than enthusiastic about going. I had an overwhelming sense of dread that I couldn't explain.

When we first made the decision to go to Vegas again, I jumped the gun by offering to drive, which I later regretted. Pixie was leaving a few days early with her boyfriend; Phil. Spencer was depending on me to drive because she recently had knee surgery. Not wanting to flake on Spencer, I put on a happy face and assumed my anxiety was based on my dad's health.

Some people would call my reluctance ESP or a sixth sense. Whatever it was, I should've listened to it and stayed home. The Vegas trip turned out to be a complete shit show.

To save money, Spencer and I shared a room with Pixie, Phil, and a few of Pixie's girlfriends from high school. We found a dingy, affordable hotel off the Las Vegas Strip. After arriving at the hotel and having a few cocktails, we took a cab to the Strip and that's when everything went downhill.

As we made our way through the crowd that packed Las Vegas Blvd., my ass was grabbed by some asshole within minutes. I was bitching about that when Pixie ran into some guys she knew from college. Her college friends were wasted, but she seemed excited to see them.

"Pictures! Pictures!" Pixie yelled.

When I tried to take a picture of them, one of the guys kept poking at Pixie and trying to grab her ass. She smacked him upside the head and told him to stop, which he did for a few moments. But as we stood there talking with them he started poking at her sides again. She didn't tell the guy to stop, so Phil thought she liked the attention, got angry off and stormed off.

Pixie went after Phil. Pixie's high school girlfriends went after her, and I went after all of them with Spencer hobbling behind as fast as she could on her bad knee.

Phil quickly disappeared in the crowd, and Pixie was reasonably upset. The plan was to start walking back to the hotel and catch a cab on the way. Poor Spencer was in a lot of pain from her knee and couldn't walk any longer. She stayed at a nearby parking lot with the plan of one of us driving back to get her. And just as we came to that agreement, we heard a roar from the Las Vegas Strip, happily welcoming in the year of 1997.

We weren't having any luck getting a cab as we walked back to the hotel. I called Phil from my cell phone and was surprised he answered. He was already back at the hotel, so I told him to come get us. He said he couldn't. Pixie took her father's car to Vegas, and he wasn't comfortable driving it. He was also drunk and didn't want to get pulled over. We ended up walking the entire way back to the hotel, which took well over an hour.

Pixie didn't want to drive her dad's car to get Spencer because she had been drinking. Nobody did. We all had been drinking. It wasn't my ideal scenario, but Spencer was in a desolate area where cabs were nonexistent. I couldn't leave her there. I reluctantly got in my car and spent the entire drive, praying I wouldn't get pulled over. I didn't, thank god. When Spencer got in the car she was furious. She didn't say a word to me on the drive back to the hotel.

When we came back to our hotel room, the tension was so thick you could've doused it in A1 sauce and cut it with a steak knife. No one said a word to each other. I grabbed my sleeping bag, curled up on the floor near a small refrigerator and hoped I would fall asleep quickly. I couldn't wait until the morning so Spencer and I could get the hell out of there.

The vibe was mildly better in the morning, although words were sparse between everyone. Spencer mumbled just enough to indicate she wanted to leave immediately. We grabbed our things and barely said goodbye to anyone when we left.

While I drove us back to L.A., the feeling of dread I had before the trip, continued to grow. I couldn't shake that feeling that something bad happened or was going to happen.

Spencer didn't talk to me until we reached Baker, a little town about halfway between Vegas and Los Angeles. Baker was known for its landmark thermometer, which stood about 130 feet high. Both of us were hungry so we stopped at Bun Boy, a little diner by the large thermometer. It wasn't until our waitress brought our drinks that Spencer broke her silence about the night before.

As we spoke, we realized we weren't mad at each other. We were frustrated with the overall situation and how everything went down the night before. I also shared the feelings of dread that had been plaguing me. I thought maybe Keith's drummer passed away while we were gone. It was the only thing I could think of to explain the strange sense of sorrow I felt.

After filling our bellies with a decent lunch, we got back on the road. I got home around 7:00 pm. I was so exhausted from a crappy night's sleep that I went straight to bed.

I was asleep for about an hour or so when the house phone rang and woke me up. For some reason, I didn't go back to sleep. I was half awake and puzzled by the strange things my mom was saying to the person on the other line. I climbed out of bed and went to the kitchen to ask her what was going on.

"Mom, who's that?" I asked, half asleep.

"It's your Aunt Rose. She's with your dad," my mom replied, somberly.

As a writer, there are no words I can think of to express the look in my mother's eyes when she said those words to me. The best way I can describe it is a mixture of confusion, fear and sorrow. It was a look I never saw from her before. I stood there waiting for her to explain her odd demeanor, but she said nothing. That's when I knew something wasn't right with my dad.

"What's wrong with dad?" I asked with a lump in my throat.

My mom looked away from me and continued talking to my Aunt Rose.

"You shouldn't tell anyone else until we know what happened," she said to my aunt.

My heart dropped. I knew why I had been having those feelings of dread.

I've never experienced shock like that before. I felt like the life was sucked out of me as I stared at my mom, waiting for an answer. An answer she didn't immediately give me but already knew.

I didn't scream. I didn't cry. My emotions were frozen and everything became quiet. I felt like I was living in a vacuum and everything around me was moving in slow motion. I couldn't hear any background noise or the sound of my mother's voice.

I turned away from my mom and slowly walked down the hallway to my bedroom. I calmly picked up the phone and called Lucy.

"Uhh hello?" she asked, jokingly.

"Hi. It's me," I said in a monotone voice.

"What's wrong?" she asked.

I took a deep breath, and when I exhaled, I said, "Dad is dead."

Twenty minutes later, Lucy and Tim pulled up to my house and we went to my dad's apartment. The police were there with my Aunt Rose.

"They're just waiting for the coroner to get here. He has to confirm the death before we can move the body. It looks like he may have had a heart attack," she said.

The coroner arrived a few minutes later. He

needed a family member to accompany him into my dad's bedroom where his body was. It was strictly a liability thing to have a family member witness the removal any jewelry my dad had on. Lucy was a wreck. I knew she couldn't go in there. I also didn't want my Aunt Rose in there either. There was something weird about the way she was acting that didn't sit well with me. I calmly said I would be the witness.

I followed the coroner into my father's bedroom. My dad was laying face first on the bed with his right arm clutched across his chest. There was a full cup of coffee sitting on a nightstand beside his bed along with a book. His slippers were neatly placed beside his bed.

Rigor mortis was setting in as the medical workers pulled rings off of my father's stiff fingers. They wrapped him in white sheets and placed him on a gurney. I stood at the doorway of his bedroom while they wheeled him into the living room and out of the apartment. When his body passed by Lucy, she broke down and collapsed into Tim's arms.

My Aunt Rose approached me when I walked into the living room. She mentioned something about rings belonging to my dad and how he always wanted her to have them.

I should have been disgusted that she was digging through my dead father's pockets, but I was numb. I wasn't sad or angry. I was nothing. I felt nothing. I looked right through my Aunt Rose without saying a word and walked over to Tim and Lucy.

When I came home that night, I didn't cry. I didn't cry the following night either. On the third day after my dad passed away, I woke up to the most excruciating back pain I've ever had in my life.

The only position that allowed relief was flat on my back with no pillows under my head. Turning my head to the side was painful. It felt like a cramp that started from my neck and trailed along my spine to my tailbone.

I didn't know what to do. I had always been considerably healthy and never dealt with back pain before. I hadn't done anything strenuous recently that would explain a back sprain. I told my mom. She gave me a few Advil, but it did nothing. After another day of back pain with no relief in sight, I told her I should go to the hospital. That's when she sat down on my bed to have a little chat.

She wanted to talk about my dad. I didn't want to. She also noticed I hadn't cried since he passed away. I told her I was afraid to. I felt if I started crying I wouldn't stop. That's when she came up with a theory about my back pain.

She told me about the mind-body connection. I wasn't allowing myself to grieve over the death of my father, so it was coming out in the form of physical back pain. I was skeptical, but everything she said made perfect sense. I had no history of back pain or any back issues whatsoever. Yet within a few days of losing my dad, I was completely debilitated.

She said I had to let out my grief, whether it be crying, talking to someone or punching a wall. I needed to find an outlet to release the overwhelming grief I was feeling. I told her I would try. I had to. My dad's funeral was the following morning.

When I went to bed that night, I tried to find something funny to watch. I was afraid of facing the fact that my dad was gone. I had an immense sense of hopelessness and emotional pain that I never felt before. I didn't know how I was going to survive without him. Not that I was going to kill myself, but I understood the meaning of when people say you can die over a broken heart. I knew that losing a parent was a part of life that any child should expect. I heard that a million times before, but that rule applied to OTHER people, not me.

I couldn't find anything I wanted to watch, so I closed my eyes and lay in bed. I thought of all the things I stressed about for the last few months. Mainly things like work, feuding friends and being dumped by Keith. They seemed so trivial. Work was nothing; I could always find another job. Whoever had a beef with each other could resolve it on their own, and no man could ever break my heart the way my father did when he died. Sure, it was a different kind of love, but there would be future boyfriends. I would never have another father.

I also thought about how my dad and I used to build stuff together when I was little. The events leading up to my parent's divorce and how we were estranged during the few years he was married to Pamela. It had been about a year since she passed. We were just starting to mend the relationship that was strained during the time he was with her. I thought about his laugh and the smell of Old Spice cologne that he wore. But most importantly, the last few words we said to each other before I left for Vegas.

He told me to have fun and handed me a few rolls of quarters to gamble with. He also jokingly said I had to split any of my winnings with him. Before he walked out the door we hugged goodbye, and he told me he loved me. I said I loved him too. That last memory of us together is what made me finally break down.

I can't remember a time when I've cried so hard. I understood the grief that drives people over the edge. When they're faced with an intense amount of crippling, emotional pain and turn to drugs in order to cope. That wasn't an option for me. My family was suffering enough. I could never be that selfish and put them through something like that after losing my dad.

I cried for what seemed like hours. I have no

memory of when I fell asleep, but I do remember having a vivid dream of my dad that night.

I was sitting in a tree by the pool at Barnes Park, close to where I grew up. The tree overlooked a pavilion where my family was eating and dancing. These were things I did in real life. I used to go to that park with my dad's side of the family all the time.

But going back to my dream, I was completely free from back pain while I sat in the tree. My dad appeared beside me, sitting on the same branch I was. I didn't have to look to know it was him. I knew it was him. I could feel his presence and smell the faint scent of his cologne. I took a deep breath and put my head on his shoulder.

"I know this is a dream. It's not real," I said, watching our family members in the pavilion.

He clutched one my hands into both of his and said, "You're okay. Everything's going to be okay."

I got choked up and muttered out the words, "Dad, I don't think I am. I'm so scared."

He didn't seem phased by my words or heightened emotions. He laughed them off as he always did. Without missing a beat he said, "Of course you'll be okay."

We didn't say much after that. I kept my head on his shoulder and held his hands as we watched our family enjoying themselves. My hair tussled around from the warm summer breeze, and with one sudden gust I was overwhelmed by the scent of my dad's cologne. Despite how real everything felt around me, I knew it was a dream, and I didn't care. I wanted to enjoy every single moment I had with my dad. I was fine not waking up for a while. I also hoped it wouldn't be the last time my dad would visit me in my dreams.

When I woke the next morning, my back felt

considerably better. I wasn't functioning at 100%, but it was enough relief for me to deal with the pain and get through the services.

My father was given a traditional military funeral for his service in the U.S. Army during the Korean War. I sat with my mom and sisters as the guard of honor signaled the firing of the volley shots, followed by the folding of the American flag that was draped over his coffin.

After the funeral, I spoke with one of my older cousins, and she told me some fun stories about my dad I never heard before. When I cracked a joke about some of the things she mentioned, she laughed and said, "Oh *mija*, that sounds like something your dad would say."

It was the best compliment I could have ever asked for. That's when I knew my dad would never be completely gone from my life. His sense of humor would influence every joke I would ever tell. He would also be right in the mirror anytime I looked at myself because we had the same nose. Call it a 'spirit', or 'energy', or whatever you want, I knew nothing could part us, though it seemed to.

As each day went by following my dad's funeral, I continued to grieve. I would cry a little less each day, and within a few weeks I was free of all back pain.

About a month or so had passed since my dad's funeral. I was slowly starting to feel better about things, but I remained in a bit of a fog. I was going through the motions of getting up, going to work, coming home and eating. But I was a robot set on autopilot. There was nothing in my life that excited me or made me happy. I needed something to snap me back to reality. Something that would let me know that life, however painful it may be, would continue after the death of my father.

After another mundane day at work, I came

home to a message from Spencer, asking if I wanted to go out that evening. She wanted to grab a drink where we could chat. I didn't want to go out, but I had dodged everyone's calls for weeks. I knew I couldn't hide from the world forever.

Spencer and I went to a dive bar near Hollywood and Highland called Powerhouse. I was halfway through my decompression session when Dexter, the host of my disastrous 20th birthday party, approached us.

Dexter was there with his friend, Jason. Upon introductions, they moved to our table and hung out with us for the rest of the evening.

Jason and Dexter were perfect company that night. It was just what I needed, a mellow night with good people. I hadn't seen much of Dexter over the last four years. But he was always a nice guy, and I was glad to be back in touch with him.

After that night, I slowly began to come out of my cloud of depression. I started to go out a little more here and there with Spencer, and we added Dexter to our social crew. We would meet up with him on weekends at different pubs, go out to dinner, and have barbecues at his house.

While I made my way back to the land of the living, I found myself thinking a lot about my friend, Faye. I hadn't heard from her in a long time. Not since months earlier when she called from a rehab center in Rosemead, about five minutes away from my house.

I was surprised when Faye called me from rehab. I didn't know she was that bad off. Based on her frustration with being there, I knew it wasn't her idea. I'm guessing it was her parents.

When I arrived at the medical center, I had to sign in and be searched before I could see Faye. After going through security, I was sent outside to a patio area with park style picnic tables. I took a seat at one of them and waited. Faye walked out a few minutes later, casually dressed in a t-shirt, jeans and sneakers.

Seeing her in civilian clothes was a rarity. She usually wore a fresh face of makeup, and a perfectly accessorized outfit with ample cleavage. Regardless, she still looked like my beautiful Faye. I welcomed her with a big hug, although I wanted to choke her for getting mixed up with a junkie like her boyfriend, Ren.

I hesitated on giving her a piece of my mind. I knew yelling at her wasn't the answer. I'm sure her parents did enough of that. I told her I was glad she was in rehab and should make the most of her time there. She couldn't stand it and said that Ren was going to get her out of there before she completed her stay.

Hearing her say that set me off. I grilled her about staying in rehab and to stop looking at it like a prison sentence. I also said she should use her time there to clear her head about things and most importantly be away from HIM.

She smiled sweetly, said I worried too much and that everything would be fine. I knew it wouldn't be.

"You better stay here and get through this. Aside from Spencer and Pixie, I don't have any close girlfriends," I said.

"Well, you have me," she said, optimistically.

"Yeah and look where you are."

We started laughing.

The reality of her situation wasn't funny but it was a lighthearted joke. While we laughed, I realized it had been a long time since we had a good, hearty chuckle together.

My visit with Faye lasted about an hour. I lived down the street and told her I would come back to visit anytime she wanted. After exchanging a big hug, Faye smiled and said she would call me in a few days to set up another visit, but she never did. That was the last time I saw Faye. I heard through the grapevine that

Ren took her out of rehab shortly after I went to see her. They supposedly took off to Mexico and got married.

Spencer and I had just arrived at Dexter's house when a friend called to tell me that Faye passed away. She died a few weeks earlier, and the details were fuzzy on what took place.

Our mutual friend told me she died from a heroin overdose. I called another friend to confirm that story, and was told she died from a head injury after hitting her head on a sink after shooting up. Regardless of the circumstances, Faye was gone and sadly, days before her 21$^{st}$ birthday.

I was angry I didn't hear about it earlier because I would have gone to the services. I found out later that Faye's parents didn't tell any of her friends. Having her Hollywood friends there would have been a slap in the face. I was insulted to be lumped in with her junkie friends, but I understood where her parents were coming from.

A couple of weeks later, I went to visit Faye at Hollywood Forever Cemetery. I left her flowers and said a final goodbye to my beautiful friend.

*WALKING CONTRADICTION*

# 3

# EMOTIONAL LIMBO, AFFAIRS, AND MORE ARRESTS

In the haze of losing my father, Faye, and Dizzy within a two-year period, I found comfort in hanging out with Dexter, despite some of our differences. I know that sounds shallow and don't get me wrong, he was a great guy, but there were a few things that irked me about him.

For one, he dressed like a hippie. He always wore shorts, Birkenstocks and tie-dye shirts. He had long, brown hair that he tied back in a ponytail and was a fan of bands like Phish, The Grateful Dead, and Rush, who I collectively couldn't stand. The thing that bothered me the most was how he bragged about having money.

Dexter was a special effects producer for Paramount Pictures. He proudly fluffed his feathers about that title and his six-figure salary, which didn't compare to those of us scraping by on $30,000 a year.

Despite those minor issues, I did enjoy hanging out with Dexter and so did Spencer. But as the weeks passed, our group outings turned into solo adventures with Dexter, and I found myself having relationship déjà vu from two years prior.

Like Randall, Dexter was a nice guy and we had a lot of fun together. But I didn't understand why it couldn't stay that way. Why did I allow these friendships to go in a physical direction? Especially when I knew it would lead to a relationship I didn't want to be in?

I thought about my disastrous dating history and tried to look at the situation objectively. Despite Dexter's financial boasting and choice in music, he was a stable guy. He was also ambitious, smart and funny. Overall, he was good on paper and a faithful boyfriend who made a great income. He also just bought a house and wanted kids. Taking those things into consideration, I told myself I could probably fall in love with him if I gave it a shot. Granted, I just turned 24 and Dexter had five years on me. I was light-years away from wanting a family, but I hoped that would change over time.

Dexter lost interest in going out when we started dating. All he wanted to do was smoke pot and hang out at home. He had a big house with a built-in bar and barbecue, so he found no reason to spend money on going out when he could throw parties at his place. That sounded great on holidays or for someone in their 40s, but I was barely in my 20s. Unless I was sick, staying home every night, especially on the weekends was completely out of the question for me.

Toward the last few months of our relationship, we started bickering over the silliest things. His biggest issue was the high volume of evenings I went out by myself.

One of my main hangouts in Hollywood was the Dragonfly. Taime Downe of Faster Pussycat was promoting a night there called The Pretty Ugly Club. He also ran the Cathouse back in the mid to late '80s. Like it's predecessor, The Pretty Ugly Club was a bar with live acts. It wasn't a snooty Hollywood club where people stood around, checking each other out. It was a rock-and-roll dive where all my friends played and hung out, so of course I went there every Wednesday night.

The more I went out without Dexter, the more pressure it put on our relationship. I was holding onto the ridiculous idea that I could make things work and eventually fall in love with him. That's when I met Cole.

Cole was the former guitar player for an old school Sunset Strip band called Warface. We knew many of the same people in Hollywood, but we were never friends until meeting at The Pretty Ugly Club.

I was standing by a fountain on the patio with Spencer when Cole walked up and said hello to her. He had bright, blue eyes and short, spiky black hair. He was exactly my type, which was the polar opposite of Dexter. Although Cole and Dexter were acquaintances, Cole wasn't hesitant when it came to flirting with me. After a cocktail or two I found myself flirting back, and that's when I knew I had to break up with Dexter.

I had never cheated on a boyfriend, and I wasn't about to start. I knew the issues I was having with Dexter weren't his fault. They weren't mine either. They were the result of two, incompatible people.

After a long night of flirting with Cole, I went home and passed out. When I spoke with Dexter the next day, I told him I felt sick and was going to stay home for the next few days, even though I was healthy as a horse. I needed a few days to build up some courage because the next time I saw him, I was going to break up with him.

I went to Dexter's a few days later with my breakup speech fully memorized. I was surprised to find a backyard full of people when I arrived. He didn't tell me he was having people over. I couldn't have "the talk" with all of those people there.

I told Dexter I wasn't in the mood for a party. He said that was ironic, considering I was out almost every night. That little dig was the fire I needed to break up with him. I could break the news to him privately in his bedroom and sneak out the front door.

Just after I told Dexter I needed to talk to him alone, our friends Marla and Jax walked up to us.

"Hey guys! What are you up to tomorrow?" Marla asked.

"Nothing yet, what's going on?" Dexter asked.

"We have two extra passes for Disneyland tomorrow, do you want to come?"

"Sure! That's sounds like a lot of fun," Dexter replied.

"Well, wait. We can't," I said.

There was no reason we couldn't go. But I hoped there would be a delay in their response so I could think of an excuse.

"How come?" Marla asked, quickly.

"Um...it's just that it's the busy season right now. The park will be packed with families and tourists. I'm not a big fan of all the pushing and getting run over by strollers at theme parks."

"Oh it'll be fine. Besides, the tickets expire this weekend and we don't want them going to waste," Jax said.

"Count us in!" Dexter said.

I was in hell.

It was Saturday night, and I planned on going out after I broke up with Dexter. I know that sounds cold, but I was done with our relationship. I had been done for months. I wanted to end things immediately and move forward. One of the worst feelings for me personally, is to be stuck with someone I don't want to be around, whether that be a friendship or a relationship. Life is too short not to be happy. When I find myself in those situations, I'm not shy about getting out of them.

Now, not only was I trapped at Dexter's house for the night but also the following day at Disneyland. I thought about taking him into the bedroom and going through with my original plan, but I didn't want to humiliate him in front of his friends. He didn't deserve that. I told everyone I wasn't feeling well and secluded myself to Dexter's bedroom for the rest of the evening, grumbling to myself.

Dexter made us breakfast the following morning. Marla and Jax picked us up, and the four of us made our way to the happiest place on earth.

Having to spend the entire day with Dexter, knowing I would be breaking up with him that night made me feel horrible. Jax and Marla made it worse by being overly affectionate with each other. They had been dating for a few months and were in honeymoon mode, while I brushed my hand away the few times Dexter tried to touch mine.

The day finally came to an end and we were dropped off at Dexter's house. I was relieved the day was over but not looking forward to the night ahead of me. When we walked in the front door I told him I needed to talk to him.

I bluntly said that things weren't working out with us. They hadn't for a while and suggested we break up or at least spend some time apart.

He looked sad and couldn't understand why I was throwing away the last year and a half of our relationship. I reiterated that it wasn't working and we spent too much time arguing over petty things. Something had to be done.

"You should think about what you're doing and not make a quick decision," he said.

"I have thought about it. I've thought about it for months. I think this is best. You deserve to be with someone who will love you unconditionally. I don't want you to waste anymore time with me," I replied.

He wouldn't take no for an answer. He said we had a long day and shouldn't make any major decisions about our relationship that night. I felt bad, so I relented and went home.

He sent me an email the next day and asked how I felt about things. I told him I hadn't changed my mind and felt it was best that we break up. He responded only with a date and time when I could pick up my things from his house.

I went to Dexter's house on the day and time he mentioned in his email. He was nowhere to be found. I grabbed the few items of clothes I kept there and threw my set of house keys on the kitchen counter before leaving.

I would love to say that Cole and I had a torrid affair filled with weeks of hot rebound sex, but that never happened. Strangely, the flirting dissipated shortly after my breakup with Dexter, and we ventured into the friend zone.

After my breakup with Dexter, I needed to rejuvenate. I had worked as a secretary at Arlen for the last five years and was burned out. I quit and flooded the job market with my resume. I also contacted the temporary employment agencies I previously signed up with. It wasn't long before I was bouncing around jobs in the Valley and downtown Los Angeles. Someone needed a secretary for a few days; another would need an assistant for a few weeks or months. I was making a somewhat steady income and couldn't be happier. Not only did I have spending money, but it was also the longest span I had without a boyfriend in ten years. That didn't last long.

A few months into my blissful freedom, I met an actor named Jake. Jake was a friend of Pixie's who she brought to The Pretty Ugly Club one night. He was a farm boy from Omaha, another one with blue eyes and dark hair. We hit it off instantly and I found myself in another long-term relationship.

I felt more optimistic about my relationship with Jake than the others because we had more in common. For one, he was obsessed with *Star Wars* and we both collected action figures. We spent most of our time dork hunting at comic book stores and conventions looking for hidden treasures.

We jumped into that relationship headfirst. Within six months of dating, we moved into a small townhouse in Studio City together.

I won't list details of what transpired during my relationship with Jake. It was nothing out of the ordinary or remotely exciting. The juicy stuff didn't happen until we broke up in late 2001.

As we rolled into the new millennium, I had recently completed another temp job and suddenly found myself without work. Jake suggested I go with him to an open casting call for a show on the *Fox* network. They were booking extras that looked like high school students for the 2nd season of a show called *Boston Public*. I didn't have anything to lose and some income was better than nothing, so I agreed to go.

A few days after we went to the open casting, I got a call that I booked the gig! Not too shabby, considering I was almost 27. Jake didn't get booked but he took the snub in stride.

I assumed the show was filmed at one of the many large studios in Hollywood. Fox Studios would make sense, or maybe the Paramount lot. That bubble was burst when my booker, Sandra, told me I would be commuting to Raleigh Studios in Manhattan Beach. Manhattan Beach, although beautiful, was an hour commute from my place, if not more.

On my first day of working at *Boston Public*, I arrived early to take a walk around the Raleigh Studios lot. David E. Kelley was the king of primetime television during that time. He had several shows running simultaneously like *The Practice*, *Ally McBeal*, and of course *Boston Public*, all of which were filmed at Raleigh Studios.

After taking a brief stroll by various stages, I walked back to find the production office for *Boston Public* when I noticed Peter MacNicol walking in my direction.

Peter was an actor on *Ally McBeal*. The first thing that came to mind was his character in *Ghostbusters II*. I wanted to yell out a quote from the movie but decided against it. Getting kicked off the lot for heckling an actor wasn't how I wanted to start my first day on *Boston Public*.

When I walked into the small lobby of the production office, I noticed two, large dressing rooms to my left and right with people scattered about. Some were reading books, while others slept or listened to music on their iPods.

In the corner of the lobby was a small desk. A woman with a slicked back ponytail sat down and waved me over. She introduced herself as Bella and said she was the wrangler for the extras on *Boston Public*. I asked her what the two rooms were for. She said they were 'holding' areas for us extras when we weren't on stage filming. After filling out some paperwork, she told me to take my clothing to a wardrobe trailer and get an outfit approved for the day.

I had bright, fire engine red streaks in my hair at the time, and when the wardrobe girl saw me she said I would make a perfect 'dungeon kid'. I never watched the show before, so I asked her what they were.

"'Dungeon kids' are the problem kids on the show. They've been kicked out of normal classes and sent to a classroom in the basement known as 'the dungeon'. Nicky Katt plays the teacher assigned to the 'dungeon kids'," she replied, informatively.

"It isn't a far cry from my real life experience in high school," I said, sarcastically.

The wardrobe girl dressed me in a plaid skirt, fishnets, combat boots and a tight, long sleeve black shirt. She also gave me a studded dog collar and suggested I wear black lipstick. I gathered my things and happily accepted my role as a 'dungeon kid' of fictional Winslow High School in Boston.

I finished getting ready and walked back to one of the holding rooms. That's when I met Quincy, a fellow 'high school' extra. He was gay, black and fierce. He told you the truth to your face but did it with witty humor, so it made whatever critique he was giving you a bit easier to swallow.

Quincy introduced me to some of the other 'high school' extras he knew. I found it funny that most of us were well into our 20's and getting away with playing high school students. Some of the kids were legit, struggling actors. Others had part time jobs and did extra work as a means to make a little money on the side.

He put the extras into two categories. There were show regulars like him, and newbies who usually worked a day or two and were never heard from again. He was the self-appointed welcoming committee to all the new 'high school' students. It made sense considering he had been on the show since the first season and knew almost everyone.

I also met a girl named Pandora who was another show regular. She was originally from Istanbul but had the faintest hint of an accent. We hit it off immediately and she would become one of my closest friends.

While I talked with Quincy and Pandora, we were called to go on set. We walked through a large set of double doors, just outside our holding rooms that led to the stage where the show was filmed.

The soundstage they filmed *Boston Public* on was massive. The entire stage was built to look like the inside of an old, East Coast school. The base of the set was a long corridor with fully functioning classrooms and stairwells. The stage also had an attendance office, a foyer, a teacher's lounge and offices for the actors who played the schools Principal and Vice Principal.

The first scene we filmed was in the main corridor. It was a conversation between the Vice Principal, played by Anthony Heald, and a new addition to the cast, Jeri Ryan, who played a lawyer turned teacher.

Bella took the extras off to the side and gave each kid specific instructions on where and when to walk. She wanted me to start in the foyer, behind Anthony and Jeri, then have me walk into the Attendance Office.

I walked to my starting spot in the foyer and leaned against a pillar. Jeri was standing nearby and casually asked about my dog collar and other accessories I was wearing as part of my 'Goth' outfit. She was so beautiful with her big, blue eyes and coiffed, blond hair. I'm surprised she spoke to me. I looked like a serial killer.

This was Jeri's first major show since leaving *Star Trek: Voyager* where she played the hottest Borg in the universe. She set the dork world on fire, as well as the loins of some of the extras on set. I noticed a few of the 'high school' guys staring at us while we talked. When we wrapped that scene about an hour later, they jumped on me like a bunch of gossiping hens and asked what it was like to talk to the sultry Seven of Nine.

While I spoke with Jeri, Anthony Heald approached us and said good morning. He introduced himself to me as Tony, asked my name and shook my hand. Considering they were main actors on the show, I was surprised at how nice and outgoing they were with me. I was a measly extra. They had no reason to make conversation with me, especially since I looked like a lunatic.

We were about to start filming, so I took my place behind Jeri and Anthony. A prop guy quickly shoved a couple of schoolbooks in my hands and ran off. We did a few takes of that particular scene, and I darted off into the Attendance Office each time, exactly as I was instructed to do by Bella.

And those are the basics of being an extra on a TV show. You go where they tell you to go, and you sit in holding until you're needed or sent home.

After completing a successful first day on set, I was called to go back the next day. I would continue going back to the set of *Boston Public* over the course of the next few months. Sometimes as much as three or four times a week. The scenes I filmed in the 'dungeon class' with my fellow students usually resulted in us throwing things at each other and running around the classroom like lunatics. It was a blast. I even scored a day player role when the schools' debate class battled a few kids from the 'dungeon class'. For those not familiar with the term, a 'day player' is a fancy word for a temporary actor who isn't part of the permanent cast. Although it was a nonspeaking role, it was a significant bump in my salary for the day. I also received a SAG voucher, and they gave me my own character name, Becky Mayron. Sure, the name lacked imagination, but I was a 'day player'. That meant I could eat from the actor's buffet, which was significantly better than the scraps they gave the extras.

Hanging out with Quincy, Pandora, and the rest of the extras on the show each week was a blast. But most of the excitement took place off set. The show should have put hidden cameras in the holding rooms and stage because the stories going on there were juicier anyway. Not only were some of the extras hooking up with each other, but also cast members were hooking up with the crew. It was like being in high school all over again. I found the debauchery amusing until I got caught up in my own scandal involving one of the actors on the show.

While I enjoyed my time on *Boston Public*, things began to dwindle between Jake and me. There were no arguments; we just weren't having any kind of communication, vertically or horizontally. We had become roommates who slept in the same bed and split the bills, rather than being an actual couple. He was preoccupied with auditions and getting his web design business off the ground, while I was working long hours on *Boston Public*. That's when I set eyes on one of the newest 'teachers' to join the main cast named Andrew Milano.

Andrew had big, brown eyes and long, wavy black hair that touched his chin. The first time I saw him was on set. Bella paired me with Quincy to walk down the main corridor during Andrew's first scene. When we passed a particular classroom door, that was Andrew's cue to walk into the hallway and speak with the school principal, played by Chi McBride.

Sometime around the second or third take, I caught Andrew looking at me between shots. Noticing how handsome he was, I reciprocated by looking back.

Quincy raised his eyebrow and said, "Ooooh girl...I KNOW you're not trying to be all up on the new teacher! Where's your man at?"

"Sshhh!! I'm not UP on any one, and he's not

technically a teacher anyway," I replied.

"You know what I mean," he said with his eyebrow still raised.

We did a few more takes, then wrapped that scene and broke for lunch. I walked with Quincy and Pandora next door to grab food. After stuffing ourselves with chicken and other goodies at Boston Market, we walked back to the production office. Some kids were sleeping in the holding rooms; others were sitting on the ground playing cards or in a corner reading a book. Quincy and Pandora wanted to take a nap, so I went outside to grab some air. I sat on a curb in front of the production office and began scribbling in my journal.

I had written a few sentences about how cute I thought Andrew was when I heard someone walk up behind me.

"Hey, how's it goin?" Andrew asked as he lit up a cigarette.

I leaned my arms over my writing and replied, "Pretty good, how are things with you?"

He took a seat next to me on the curb and said, "I can't complain. I just wrapped for the day so I'm heading out soon."

I casually closed my journal as we introduced ourselves. Andrew was originally from Harlem. It was his first time in California. The show was putting him up at a hotel around the corner during production. He also mentioned his acting background was primarily in theatre and how excited he was that this was his first, major TV role.

We spoke for a few minutes until Bella walked out and told Andrew he was needed on set for a re-take. She also needed ten high school students and told me to get in there too. Andrew and I continued our conversation as we walked onto the sound stage, and the casual glances between us resumed while he redid his scene.

When we finished reshooting Andrew's scene, I was wrapped for the day along with the rest of the extras. I gathered my things from holding and was halfway to the parking lot when Quincy caught up to me and started grilling me about Andrew.

He pointed his finger at me and said, "You are a HEATHEN. And don't act like you don't know what I'm talking about either."

"Heathen? Who uses that word anymore?" I said, laughing.

"Gurrll…you're asking for trouble if you get involved with that teacher."

"I'm not getting involved with anyone. All we did was talk, and stop calling him a teacher. It's creepy!"

I said my goodbyes to Quincy and wondered if he was right. Maybe I should've been distancing myself from Andrew. I was vulnerable, and it didn't help that Andrew was a good-looking guy giving me attention I wasn't getting at home.

Overall, I wasn't too concerned. I never cheated on a boyfriend before because I've always had a black and white view on infidelity. That being, if you feel like you're getting to a point where you're going to cheat, then break up with that person. Who has the time or energy to go behind someone's back and hide such a mess? But more importantly, why would you hurt someone you love? If you've fallen out of love, do your mate a favor and break up with them. Don't drag them through the dirt.

After some careful thought, I felt the flirting with Andrew would blow over in a few days. But as we continued to talk on set, my feelings for him grew stronger, while my relationship with Jake was washing itself out to sea.

Jake and I were long overdue on having "the

talk". I knew it needed to be done. I was packing up to leave the studios when he called and asked when I was coming home. He wanted to talk and cancelled a meeting to stay home and meet me. That's when I knew it was going to be THAT talk.

When I opened the door to the townhouse we shared, Jake was sitting on the couch, watching TV. He put the TV on mute as I walked into the living room. I put my things down on a coffee table in front of me and took a seat on the couch next to him.

His web design business wasn't building up the momentum he had hoped. He blamed it on living in Los Angeles and having too much competition. He felt he would be better off in a smaller town, or more specifically, his hometown of Omaha.

"So you're moving back to Omaha to get your business off the ground?" I asked.

"Yes. My family is there, and I already have a job waiting for me at the local theatre until business picks up. I think I've got a better chance at getting the business off the ground there than here," he replied.

I knew that meant we were breaking up, but I had to ask. I didn't want to leave any room for ambiguity.

"Okay…so…where does that leave us?" I asked.

"I'm guessing you don't want to move to Omaha?"

"Of course not. My family is here, my life is here."

"But other than your family, you don't have anything keeping you here. You don't have a steady job, you're not in school."

"Wow you're making this breakup easier by the minute aren't you?" I said, sarcastically.

"I didn't mean it that way, but you don't. There's nothing solid keeping you here."

"No offense, but I don't care to live in Omaha.

My life is out here with my family and friends. That's a pretty 'solid' reason to me. I have better job opportunities in Los Angeles than I do in Nebraska."

"So we're breaking up then?" he asked.

"Yeah I guess so," I replied.

It was the strangest breakup I ever experienced. I felt like I should cry or be dramatic and throw something, but I didn't feel particularly upset. To be honest, I was a bit hungry.

"Okay, this is just weird," I said, bluntly to break the awkward silence.

"I'm glad you said that. I didn't know what to say either," he replied.

We both shared a snicker and that's when I felt a little sad. It was Jake's humor that initially attracted me to him; only it had been buried under his business sense for the last few months.

He was moving back to Omaha at the end of the month and gave notice to our landlord. I wanted to stay in the townhouse but I couldn't afford it on my own. He was also going to Omaha in a few days to look at apartments. While we sorted out the final details of our breakup, I was surprised at the lack of tension between us. There didn't seem to be any bad blood once we came clean about how we felt.

Jake flew to Omaha the following weekend, and I was excited to have the townhouse to myself. I was obsessed with a synth rock band called Orgy who had a big show in Hollywood that weekend. After some minor finagling, I scored a spot on their guest list.

I went to the show by myself and ran into a bunch of old Hollywood friends like Mandie from Glamour Punks. But shortly after Orgy played, I wasn't feeling well, so I decided to head home. I was saying my goodbyes when Mandie asked for a ride. I said sure, and he followed me to my car.

We were sitting at a red light on the corner of

Hollywood and Highland when I realized I forgot to turn my headlights on. I turned them on, and shortly after I made my left turn onto Highland, the police pulled me over in front of a donut shop near Franklin Avenue.

The officer asked why it took so long for me to turn my lights on. I explained it was simple forgetfulness and it truly was. Sure, I had a few drinks but forgetting to turn my lights on was something I did when I was sober. I didn't think it was a big deal until he told me to get out of the car.

I performed a few sobriety field tests and failed them miserably. They arrested me and put me in the back of a patrol car.

Mandie was dating a stripper at the time named Macey. She was about to get off work, so he said he would call her.

A million thoughts went through my mind as I rode in the back of the patrol car. This was a far cry from being arrested in high school at a keg party. I wouldn't call that a legitimate arrest because I was dropped off at home for mouthing off to a cop.

I would most likely get a DUI and be charged thousands of dollars in fines. The cost of my car insurance would sky rocket. The thing I feared most was jail time. I couldn't imagine myself in jail.

I was taken to the police station on Wilcox, just south of Sunset where I was booked. They put me in a holding tank with my cuffs still on; as if I were some degenerate they didn't trust. The room was cold, the bench was hard and the heavy cuffs were digging into my bony wrists.

I sat in the tank for about an hour until I was released. I walked out to find Macey and Mandie waiting for me. I had never been so happy to see them. I told Macey I owed her one, a big one for coming to get me out. They only let me go because she was sober.

Otherwise, I would have spent the night in jail.

Macey and Mandie dropped me off at home around four in the morning. I had a restless sleep for a few hours. Not only from my arrest, but I had to move my car from Highland Avenue because of street sweeping. I called a cab around eight in the morning and although it was illegal, I hopped into my car and drove it home.

I thought about calling Jake to tell him what happened, but he wasn't my boyfriend anymore. There was nothing he could do from Omaha anyway. I also wasn't in the mood to get an earful from him or anyone. My secret wouldn't last long though. Jake came home a few days later and after checking our mail, asked why we were getting flyers and letters from DUI lawyers.

I went through the letters and fliers. There was one that stuck out from a Mr. Henry Weinberg. It was a glossy flyer with a picture of him, touting his thirty years of experience in DUI cases. He was old and Jewish. Sold.

Mr. Weinberg was able to get my DUI dropped to a lesser 'wet reckless' charge, which resulted in lesser penalties across the board. My fines were within reason and I would avoid jail time.

I didn't have the money upfront to pay for Mr. Weinberg, so I cashed in a 401k plan I had built since my days at Arlen. I earned about $10,000 and planned on letting that money grow until I was ready to buy a house. But by the time I paid taxes, court fees, and penalties for early withdrawal, not to mention my lawyer fees, I was left with almost nothing.

My driver's license was also suspended. I had to take a series of AA classes to get it back. I was also late on my car payments and hadn't paid car insurance in months. My life was in shambles both emotionally and financially.

I was due back on *Boston Public* about a week after my arrest. The first thing I thought of was seeing Andrew again. I know that's pathetic, but it was the only escape I had from everything that was crumbling around me. I was also newly single and didn't have to deal with my conscience, otherwise known as Quincy, breathing down my neck anymore.

After checking in with Bella on my first day back, I went to holding to grab some snacks. Pandora was sitting nearby reading a book while Quincy made himself a bowl of cereal. He pulled a gallon jug of Homogenized Milk from a nearby ice cooler and poured it over his Fruit Loops.

"I haven't had Vitamin D milk in ages. How do you drink that stuff?" Pandora asked.

"Let me guess? Your BONY ass drinks non-fat milk, don't you?" Quincy asked.

"Yeah, what's wrong with that?"

"That ain't nothing but gray water that's what's wrong with it. Personally, I like the milk you have to chew."

"You guys are never going to guess what happened with me and Jake," I said, interrupting the conversation.

"Hold that thought," Quincy replied. "Let me grab another box of Fruit Loops before the vultures for the 10:00 a.m. call eat all the cereal."

Quincy grabbed a small box of Fruit Loops, put it under his arm and the three of us walked outside.

I was briefing Pandora and Quincy on my breakup with Jake, when Charles, one of the crew guys on the show, walked up behind us.

"Now that you're single, don't get any ideas about Andrew," Charles said.

I panicked. I thought I did a good job of keeping my feelings for Andrew under wraps. I also wanted to kick Pandora and Quincy for not letting me know that he was walking up behind me.

"Huh? What are you talking about?" I asked, innocently.

"Oh cut the crap. We've all seen the way you and Andrew have been staring at each other for the last few weeks."

Quincy shook his finger at me and said, "See? I told your nasty ass to be more careful."

"Look, I don't care if you hook up with Andrew," Charles said. "The only reason I brought it up is because he's not here anymore."

"What do you mean he's not here anymore? Did he finish filming all his scenes for the season already?" I asked.

"No, he was fired."

"Fired? Why?" I asked.

"He wasn't cutting it. Come on, you saw him struggling the other day when we were filming the classroom scene. How many times did the director have to coach him? It's to be expected though. He's a theatre kid who's never done television before."

"So what happens now? Did the show kill off his character?" I asked.

"Nah, they recast the character and changed the name because he was Italian, and the guy they replaced him with clearly isn't."

"Who did they replace him with?" Pandora asked.

"Michael Rapaport," Charles replied.

"Michael Rapaport?" Quincy asked with a mouth full of cereal.

"Yeah, they're canning the footage with Andrew and reshooting everything with Michael," Charles replied.

I felt bad for Andrew. This was supposed to be his big break. I wanted to talk to him, but I had no way to get in touch with him. I couldn't ask Bella or anyone from production for his info. That would have been more scandalous, so I did something I had never done before. I put my female snooping skills to work and searched him out.

The first thing I did was make a list of the information I did have, which wasn't much. Aside from his first and last name, I only knew he was staying at a hotel somewhere near the studio.

I finished filming on *Boston Public* around 2:00 p.m. that day. The moment I got home, I searched for all the hotels near Raleigh Studios. I ruled out the fancier ones, the show would never put him at a five star hotel. I narrowed it down to three. I called the first two, with no luck. The Residence Inn on Sepulveda was the last on my list.

"Hello, Residence by Marriott, can I help you?" a voice said on the other line.

"Hi, can you tell me if you have an Andrew Milano staying with you?" I asked.

"Sure, let me check on that for you."

I waited for a few moments and the phone began to ring. I waited patiently, thinking the front desk had transferred me to another department when a man answered the phone.

"Hello?" the man asked.

The man sounded like Andrew.

"Helllooo?" the man asked again.

I knew it was Andrew and quickly hung up. I didn't expect them to transfer me to his room. I just wanted to know if he was staying there.

Now I had a dilemma on my hands. If I called right back he would know it was me that hung up. I thought of a simple plan and called the hotel back. Andrew answered his phone again.

"Hello?" he asked.

"Andrew?" I asked.

"Yeah, who's this?"

"It's Marisa, from *Boston Public.*"

"Oh hey! Did you just call a few minutes ago?"

"Yeah I did. Must've been a bad connection. I couldn't hear you," I said, crossing my fingers.

"It's all good. How are ya?"

"I'm good. I wanted to say hi and see how you're doing. I just heard the news."

"I'm okay, it's kind of a long story. I'm not much of a phone person, but um…what are you doing right now?"

My heart raced.

"I'm hanging out at home, why?" I asked, casually.

"Do you feel like coming to Hermosa Beach? We can grab a drink and I'll tell you what happened."

My first instinct was to say no because I had a boyfriend. Thank god I stopped myself. I never mentioned Jake in my previous conversations with Andrew. And now that I was newly single, I wasn't going to ruin the moment by going into a long story about the breakup.

"Yeah, I'd love to! I can be there in about an hour." I replied.

After getting Andrew's hotel information, I sat back on my living room couch. Could what I was doing be considered cheating or just a mild case of bad taste? It wasn't the most ethical thing to be running into Andrew's arms before the body was cold on my relationship with Jake.

While I sat and pondered the rules of break up etiquette, Jake walked in the door. He said he was spending the weekend in Thousand Oaks with some actor friends.

I couldn't believe my luck. With Jake being gone for the weekend, I didn't have to worry about making my way home at a decent hour, or at all for that matter. Fate might as well have rented me a car and drove me out to Hermosa Beach.

Jake stayed long enough to grab a few things before he was out the door. It wasn't long before I did the same and made my way out to Hermosa Beach.

I was nervous and excited as I pulled my car into the driveway of the Residence Inn Hotel. I idled past several small buildings on the property, each holding four rooms, two on top, two on bottom. I came upon his building and found parking out front.

What transpired that evening and over the next few nights were events that belonged in a Danielle Steele novel. There was sex; there were dinners along the beach. We drank wine in his Jacuzzi and he read me short stories from *The Most Beautiful Woman in Town and Other Stories* by Charles Bukowski. I was never a fan until Andrew introduced me to that book. Bukowski would become a heavy influence on my writing style, and I ate up his books like literary, chocolate cake.

Andrew and I had a perfect setup. I would go to his hotel each day after leaving the set. To explain my nights away, I told Jake I was crashing at a friend's house, but he didn't care. He was focused on getting his things shipped back to Omaha.

And when I thought my rendezvous with Andrew was on a glorious streak, it came to a screeching halt the night before he flew back to New York.

I had just arrived at Andrew's hotel room after a long day of filming. I was usually met with a kiss and a glass of red wine, but that particular night he was oddly distant. He said he had a lot on his mind and had a phone appointment to talk with his therapist. I told him I would leave the room if he wanted, but he said I could stay. He wanted to get some fresh air and planned on strolling around the large parking lot during his one-hour session.

He grabbed his cell phone and gave me a half

smile before walking out the door. I grabbed my journal from my purse and started to scribble my concerns over his sudden change in disposition.

I assumed part of it was finances. He was fired from *Boston Public* about a week earlier, and the show stopped paying for his hotel the day after they let him go. He changed his plane ticket and extended his stay, so all costs were coming out of his own pocket. Whatever the reason, I hoped his session would go well and change his mood.

When Andrew came back in after his session, I asked if everything was okay. He said he was bummed over family problems and losing the *Boston Public* gig. I thought there was something more going on though. It felt like he didn't want me there. I knew I couldn't ignore the situation. I would have to ask that question; even though leaving the hotel was the last thing I wanted to do.

"If you're not feeling good, I can leave if you want. I really don't want to be a bother," I said, sweetly.

He paused for a moment. I felt a knot in my stomach and regretted asking him that question. We had an amazing time over the last week. I didn't want to end things badly before he went back to New York.

"It's fine, you don't have to leave," he said, unenthusiastically.

Hearing the indifference in his voice didn't make me feel any better.

His mood lifted while we ate dinner but not by much. It was uncomfortable sitting beside him when he seemed so detached, but if I went home I would be just as miserable. Funny how that room was our safe haven for the last week. Now, although we were in the same spot, we were in a completely different place.

He cracked a joke here and there while we watched a movie but it wasn't the same. There was no romance, wine drinking or reading me stories in the

Jacuzzi. Ironically, Andrew read the last short story from that book the night before. There were no more tales to be told from Bukowski or us for that matter.

I wasn't booked to work on *Boston Public* the following day, so I gave Andrew a ride to the airport. I pulled up to his terminal and we both got out of my car. He pulled the Bukowski book out of his bag and gave it to me. He wrote an inscription but told me not to read it until I got home. We exchanged a hug and kiss goodbye, then he grabbed his bags and walked away.

In situations like that, I have zero patience. I pulled into the parking lot of a nearby Taco Bell to read his inscription.

*"Marisa, I'll never read this book to another, alien or other. Never give up on your writing or lose your sense of humor. It's what makes you, YOU.*

*Maybe I'll walk into a bookstore and see yours alongside Bukowski's someday!*

*Love A"*

Things were dismal after Andrew went back to New York. Not only because of how things ended with us, but I was also broke and about to be homeless. I thought things couldn't get any worse, but they did about a week later on the morning of September 11th.

I usually listened to Howard Stern on my morning commute to Raleigh Studios. But that morning I felt like listening to music, which I did until I pulled off the freeway.

I pulled up to the security gate at Raleigh Studios and tuned in to Howard while I gave the guard my information. When I drove through the gate, I realized Howard wasn't talking. He was streaming a live news feed of a speech by President Bush. I caught the tail end of what he said, and I heard something about terrorism.

I walked up to the production office with my things and noticed a few extras outside crying. I didn't know them well, so I felt it would be inappropriate to ask why they were so upset.

I walked through the lobby and into one of the holding rooms. A few of the extras were sitting on the floor, listening to a small radio. I asked one of them what happened and they said two commercial planes hit the towers of the World Trade Center.

The thought of such a thing was beyond my comprehension. It had to be a hoax or a case of bad reporting. But when I sat down with the kids and we heard the live report of a third plane hitting The Pentagon; the reality hit me like a ton of bricks. It was also being reported that every airport in the country was being temporarily shut down until further notice.

Bella popped her in head into both holding rooms and yelled for everyone to come into the lobby. Everyone stood up and rushed into the lobby.

She said filming on all of David E. Kelley's shows would be temporarily suspended until further notice and everyone should go home right away.

Some of the kids mentioned the 405 freeway was shut down by the LAX Airport. Others claimed it was still open. I didn't know what to believe, but I didn't want to get stuck on the freeway. I mapped out a different route and took the streets home.

I left the studios immediately and what would have been a 40-minute commute turned into a 2-hour drive. Thank god Howard was on the air. I listened to him the entire way home. He chose to stay on the air to provide the latest updates for those that didn't have access to other news. Not only was he patching in other newsfeeds from different stations, but he was also taking calls from listeners who were grateful they had a place to vent their sadness and frustration. I tried phoning some of my friends in New York but I couldn't get through. I didn't know if the lines were down or completely overloaded from other people checking in with their loved ones.

Jake was in the living room watching TV when I came home. I was finally able to see the news footage that Howard spoke about for the last few hours.

Watching the planes intentionally dive into each of the Twin Towers was the most horrific sight I have ever seen in my life. It was like watching a scene from a doomsday movie. When they started to show people jumping out of the fiery buildings, I had to walk away. I grabbed my cell phone and went for a walk down my street. I was trying to catch my breath and comprehend the madness that was taking place in my beloved New York. I couldn't imagine the mindset of what those people were going through and my heart broke for each of them.

I tried to call my friends in New York again and finally got through to Dresden and Andrew. Both were safe and had the same things to say. They were sad, they were angry, and the air quality was horrific due to the debris from the buildings.

I got a call from Sandra about a week later to go back to *Boston Public*. Usually when I drove up to the security booth at the studios, I would hand over my ID, a guard would check my name off a list, and I drove right through. But on my first day back after Sept 11th, I was asked to open the trunk of my car for inspection while they checked my ID. There was another guard carrying a long pole with a mirror at the end of it, which he used to check underneath the entire perimeter of my car. Sure, it was a bit strange that security would go to such great lengths. But that's how paranoid everyone was right after the attacks took place.

On a lesser note, once the airports were operating at full capacity again, Jake moved back to

Omaha. During the time we were together, I made the mistake of opening a credit card in both our names. More than half of the $2000 incurred on our card were his charges. He promised to pay off his share once he returned to Omaha. But when I began phoning him to ask for money, he stopped returning my calls.

We were still sharing a storage unit in North Hollywood that he was paying for. It included quite a few of his *Star Wars* collectables and about 99% of my collection. We both had a key for the unit. I thought about selling his stuff if he didn't pay me back. Unfortunately, he knew me too well. When I went to the unit, I noticed the lock was different. He must have changed it before he left without telling me, or he had a friend in town do his dirty work for him.

I went to the storage manager and asked him to break the lock. When he looked at the paperwork on our unit, he said Jake never added me as an additional owner to the contract. Even though he saw Jake and I walk in there together for the last few months, legally he couldn't do anything for me. If I went to break the lock on my own it would be considered burglary.

I left Jake a voicemail and told him to forget the credit card charges. I would call it even if he gave me my stuff back from the unit. He didn't return my call, so I left him a more colorful voicemail telling him what a piece of shit coward he was for stealing my entire *Star Wars* collection. He knew how much those pieces meant to me. He didn't return that call either.

My stomach was in knots for weeks. I hated him for what he did and it was starting take a physical toll on me. That's when I knew I had to let it go. I loved that collection but they were material things. I needed to move on.

Working on *Boston Public* was fun, but it was time to find a permanent, full time job. I was only making about $50 a day. That was nowhere near what I needed to get my own apartment. I made more when I worked overtime, but those days were few and far between.

I went over a game plan with Spencer. I would be down and out for a few weeks, maybe a month tops. She had her own apartment in North Hollywood and graciously offered up her couch until I could get back on my feet.

Unfortunately, my job search wasn't going as well as I hoped. I hadn't landed a permanent job or even a temporary one. My only income was the pittance from *Boston Public*. The weeks turned into months, and I knew I was crowding Spencer. It was time to give her a break. I left her place and moved in with Lucy and Tim by Pasadena.

I can't complain though. I had my own bedroom at Lucy and Tim's house, but I hated being a burden on them. I insisted on paying for my own food, which was hard when I hadn't landed a job and would only get called onto set once a week. I had a car payment, insurance, and a cell phone bill to pay. It doesn't sound like much to most people, but I was living off of about $10-$15 of food a week, just to pay those bills. There's only so much you can do with Top Ramen, eggs, and lemon water, which were my primary meals for weeks at a time.

Shortly before *Boston Public* wrapped it's 2nd season, I landed a long-term temp job. I would be working in Koreatown doing secretarial work for an elderly southern businessman named Bubba. Bubba was outspoken and a bit harsh at times. He had a Yosemite Sam mustache and a horribly fitting blond toupee that constantly slid off his head.

It was menial work, but the job with Bubba lasted a few months. I also got in good with a temp recruiter named Eden who gave me the job. When my assignment with Bubba ended, she immediately booked me for another gig. And when that ended she got me another. Almost a year had passed since I left the townhouse. I also saved up enough money to leave Lucy and Tim's. It wasn't enough to afford a place on my own, so I moved in with a girl named Dee.

Dee was an entertainment coordinator for Kirkland Media, a public relations company that ran most of the biggest celebrity events in town. I met Dee after answering her ad on *Craigslist* for a roommate to share her 2 bed, 2 bath apartment in West Hollywood. The apartment was walking distance to all the clubs on the Strip and a fifteen-minute commute to my temp job. We got along well, and I moved in the following week.

I had been going to West Hollywood since I was 13. But living there was different than living in the Valley. There was always something going on every night of the week, and I didn't want the apartment to be a party house. Luckily, Dee and I were in agreement. She would smoke pot in her room on her days off, but that didn't bother me. I joined in from time to time. I thought all was calm in terms of my life being party central until I met Tyler.

I tried Ecstasy once before meeting Tyler, or as they called it back then, "E", but that changed once we started dating.

Tyler was a few years older and originally from Miami. He was skinny with black eyes to match his short, black hair. We met at the Rainbow one night through a mutual friend. He was into Asian culture and the Hollywood rave scene. His favorite spot was a dance club called Spundae on Santa Monica Boulevard near Highland. It was a vast change from the rock clubs I grew up going to. But I wanted to do something different, so I started going to Spundae with Tyler and doing E quite frequently. Tyler did E, K (Ketamine, an animal tranquilizer), and every other drug-abbreviated letter he could get his hands on and so did his circle of friends. I also had a feeling he was doing cocaine too.

Cocaine was still a huge no no for me. I had an unexplainable aversion to that drug. I didn't want to do it and I didn't want to date anyone that did cocaine. Tyler said he hadn't done it in a long time. I never saw it in the house, but I had my suspicions. I clearly wasn't right in the head during that time, which is why I never pushed the issue with him.

Pixie, who did have her head on straight couldn't stand Tyler and rightly so. Granted, she was with me the first time I did E at Mandie's house about a year earlier, but she thought it was a one-time thing. When I started dating Tyler it became more frequent, almost every weekend to be exact. She knew he was doing other drugs and didn't want me falling down the drug-addicted rabbit hole, which she harshly reminded me of every time I spoke to her.

I dated Tyler for nine months and the end came when I unknowingly did heroin.

Tyler and I were at Spundae one night and I had taken a hit of E. We were sitting outside with some of his crack head friends for about a half hour when it hit me. It was a wave of nausea that punched me right in the gut. I dry heaved. I took a deep breath to try and relax but I dry heaved again. I abruptly ran away from Tyler and bolted toward the girl's bathroom.

There were about ten girls in line and I ran past all of them. I told the girl who was next in line that I felt sick. She must have seen the panic on my face because she sweetly told me I could go next.

A stall opened up a few seconds later, so I ran in and leaned over the toilet. I held my hair back with one hand and put the other on one of the walls of the stall to stabilize myself.

I threw up the last two cocktails I ingested within the last hour. When I was finished, I cleaned my face and walked back to find Tyler.

"Hey, are you okay? What happened?" he asked.

"I have no idea. I just started dry heaving. I don't think its food poisoning though. Usually you feel nauseous for a few hours before you puke and this came from out of nowhere," I said.

"I bet it was the E," said Dewey, one of Tyler's crack head friends.

"But I've taken E a bunch of times and that's never happened before," I said.

"Yeah but every batch is laced with something different. Some have more speed than others and some have a bit of heroin. I'm guessing your pill was more on the dopey side," he said, informatively.

I was the only dopey thing for becoming a regular E user.

I wanted to leave Spundae, but Tyler was my ride. I didn't have money for a cab to get home, so I stayed, and while I stayed the E started to kick in.

We stayed at Spundae for another hour then went back to Tyler's. He invited his crack head friends back to his place, and because I was rolling my ass off on E, I stayed up for the party like nothing ever happened.

The hours passed, the sun came up and I started to get hungry. I hadn't looked at the clock in a while, but I assumed it was six or seven in the morning. The last of the party crew had just left, but I wasn't the least bit tired. There was probably speed in the E I had taken too. I told Tyler we should grab some breakfast. He agreed and ran off to the bedroom to change.

I grabbed my cell phone to check the time. It was just past three in the afternoon. I didn't believe it. I shut off my cell phone and turned it back on, thinking I had a bad signal.

After confirming the time of day, I was sick to my stomach. Not because of the alcohol or Ecstasy, but I had been up for almost two days straight and didn't feel the least bit tired.

I looked around Tyler's messy living room. It was filled with empty beer bottles and bags of chips. There were empty plastic cups all over the place and foam boxes of half eaten takeout all over the kitchen counters. I walked over and looked in a nearby mirror. I was disgusted. I looked like a cracked out, pile of shit. I couldn't understand how I got to that point and ended up with someone like Tyler.

I didn't want to be a crack head like him and his friends. It wasn't me and it wasn't what I wanted my life to be. I'm sure I was still under the influence of all that I consumed from the night before, but at that moment, I saw things clearly for the first time since dating Tyler.

I thought about giving him an ultimatum, but I didn't care enough about our relationship to see it through. He liked to party and would continue to do so with or without me. Sure, we cared for each other but we were never in love. The foundation of our relationship was built on partying, and I had no desire to be around him any longer, even if he was clean.

When Tyler walked back to the living room, I said I changed my mind about breakfast. I told him I didn't feel well and was going home. I could tell by the look on his face that he knew something was wrong, but I didn't want to get into it. I didn't want to deal with any of it. I just wanted to get the hell out of there.

I hugged him goodbye like everything was fine and told him we would talk later. I walked out of his apartment and promised myself I would never go back there again.

I picked up some Taco Bell on the way home, hoping it would put me into a food coma but it didn't. I wasn't able to wind down and fall asleep until about nine or ten that evening. That was the last time I ever partied with Tyler.

My roommate, Dee, noticed I was out of sorts after my breakup with Tyler. I wasn't about to fill her in on my *Trainspotting* experience, so I played it off like a standard case of break up blues. In an effort to raise my spirits, she offered to put me on the guest list for her next event.

About a week later, Dee told me she was coordinating an engagement party for musician, Dave Navarro and his hot mama actress/fiancé, Carmen Electra. The party was being held at the Astra Lounge, a little bar inside the Pacific Design Center, which was down the street from our apartment.

Dee told me I could bring a guest. I hadn't seen Pandora in a while, so I called her and she squealed with excitement. It was her first red carpet event.

The night of the party, Pandora picked me up and we went to the Astra Lounge. We pulled in the driveway and noticed there wasn't a parking lot, only valet. Most of the cars pulling up were BMW's, Mercedes, and a few Jaguars. Meanwhile, we were in Pandora's clunky Buick Skyhawk, which jerked hard into first gear and shook violently while it idled.

I didn't want to be a shallow asshole, so I stayed silent until Pandora's car suddenly backfired. We both started laughing. She said there was no way in hell she wanted to be seen in that thing and drove right back out of the driveway.

We walked up to the Astra Lounge, and I saw Dee standing out front with her clipboard. Next to her was a Step and Repeat where a gaggle of photographers climbed over each other to take pictures of celebrities as they walked down the carpet.

When we reached Dee she told us we looked great and to wait a few moments. Carmen and Dave were about to arrive. A few minutes later, they walked the red carpet and the photographers went nuts. Dave was dressed in all black. Carmen had her long, caramel locks draping down a slinky, peach-colored dress with a plunging neckline. They made their way into the Astra Lounge, and Dee told us to go ahead and walk the carpet.

The moment Pandora and I stepped onto the red carpet those cameras came down faster than a hooker's panties. It was our first Hollywood snub. We laughed it off and continued our way down the carpet and into the Astra Lounge.

Pandora and I went straight to the bar to partake in the complimentary drinks and take a look around. The music was loud and the lounge was a smorgasbord of various celebrities. Jeremy London from *Party of Five* was there, Duff McKagan from *Guns N' Roses* strolled in with his wife. Hugh Hefner and his blondtourage of seven 'girlfriends' were there too.

After mooching our first round of drinks, we ordered another. We glanced around the room for a place to sit and noticed a bench nearby where an out-of-place elderly couple was sitting. There was a vacant spot next to them, so we picked up our drinks and made our way over to the bench.

We were sipping our drinks and nibbling on appetizers when we saw Carmen and Dave walking in our direction. They approached the elderly couple, exchanging hugs and kisses with them. I didn't think anything of it until Carmen leaned over and whispered something to Dave. I was looking in a different direction, but I could feel them staring at us. I casually leaned over to Pandora.

"Are we not supposed to be sitting here?" I whispered closely in her ear.

"I don't know. I didn't see this area roped off or anything," Pandora replied.

I sipped on my drink and chatted with Pandora. Duff walked over and began talking to Dave and Carmen, but I could still feel her looking in our direction.

"I have a feeling we're not supposed to be sitting here. Can you feel her mad dogging us?" I whispered to Pandora.

"Yeah I think we should probably move," Pandora said.

We stood up, casually strolled away and found another empty bench near the front door. When we sat down, Dave and Carmen took our old seats by the elderly couple.

"How embarrassing," I said. "I wonder if they were their grandparents or something."

"Oh well, who cares. Here comes a waiter with more appetizers. I'm hungry," Pandora replied.

"Yeah I'm hungry too."

While we stuffed our faces with free appetizers, I noticed a casually dressed guy walk in with a few people and go right to the bar. Everyone else was decked out in gowns, slacks and dress shirts while the stranger wore a simple pair of jeans, sneakers and a blue Dickies jacket with a white shirt underneath.

"Ha! From the back he kind of looks like Owen Michaels," I said, jokingly.

"He does huh? But he looks way too short to be Owen," Pandora replied.

Owen Michaels was an actor on a Fox show called *Bridgepoint*. He played a corrupt police officer, and I had swooned over him for the last two years. I fantasized about what I would do if it were Owen, but I knew it couldn't be. His show filmed in Canada, and if he were in Los Angeles, I couldn't imagine why he would be at an event like that anyway.

I had just stuffed an appetizer in my mouth when the mystery man turned around with his drink. It was Owen Michaels.

"Oh my fucking god," I mumbled with my mouth full.

"You HAVE to go up to him!" Pandora squealed.

"I can't! I ate off all my lipstick!"

"Go the bathroom, fix your makeup and get back out here! Hurry!"

Owen started chatting with a heavyset gentleman beside him. I grabbed my purse and ran past him to the women's restroom as I tried to swallow the last bits of food in my mouth.

I touched up my hair and fixed my lipstick. I couldn't have been in there for more than five minutes, but Owen was gone by the time I came out. The porkly gentleman was talking to someone else.

Pandora and I took a casual stroll around the lounge so I could stalk Owen, but he was nowhere to be found.

"Talk about making an appearance and leaving. I guess it's for the best. I don't know what I would've said to him anyway," I said.

"So what do you want to do now?" Pandora asked.

"I'm still hungry, and I could use another drink. I say we keep eating and drinking as long as it's free," I said.

"I'm still hungry too," she replied.

We waved down a nearby waiter, piled a few more appetizers on our dainty napkins and continued inhaling.

# 4

# MAKING AMENDS AND THE TV STAR

**A**bout a month or so had passed since my breakup with Tyler. It felt great to have him and the drugs completely out of my system. And what better way to celebrate a new beginning than to go to a wedding? Spencer and I put on our best dresses to celebrate the wedding of Mandie to his beautiful wife-to-be, Sandy.

It was one of the best weddings I had been to, and I had gone to quite a few. But most were the result of obligation. Not to say the people getting married didn't care for each other, but most were bickering couples that had been together for years. But with Mandie and Sandy, you could feel how much they genuinely loved and cared for each other. It gave me hope that I would find love like that some day.

The wedding was also a mini reunion of sorts. A handful of the old school kids were there like Dresden, Cole, Pixie, Spencer, among others and to my surprise, Dina.

The last time I saw Dina was about eight years earlier, shortly after my falling out with Cassidy. Dina and I got into a shoving match at a party in the Valley after she called me a whore for dating Dresden. She was drunk the last time I saw her, but I didn't know if her mindset had changed toward me. I could only hope.

Shortly after the reception started, I inadvertently made eye contact with Dina. She looked at me for a few moments and started to make her way toward me. She didn't look mad, but she didn't look happy to see me either. I didn't know what to expect and before I could think of what to do, she was standing in front of me.

"I'm so sorry for all the stupid shit that happened. We were so young and it was such a long time ago. Can we just get a drink?" she asked with a smile.

"I'm glad you said that. I'm sorry too," I said as we hugged.

After picking up some drinks from the bar, we sat down at a nearby table and cracked a few jokes about our faux fight in the valley. Aside from the actual wedding itself, the best part of my night was catching up with Dina.

Through my reunited friendship with Dina, I was able to bury the hatchet with Amie as well. I was happy to mend those fences, but the one friendship I lost that bothered me the most was with Cassidy.

Cassidy was one of my closest friends back in the old Sunset Strip days. I missed her terribly through the years and always regretted how badly I handled things between us. After making things kosher with Dina and Amie, I hoped I would get the chance to make things right with her too.

Cassidy and Mandie were close. I thought I would get an opportunity to talk to her at his wedding but she was a no show. And with her still living in New York, I knew the chances of bumping into her were slim to none.

While I continued to kick myself over my lost friendship with Cassidy, having my finances take a nosedive didn't do much for my self-esteem either. My lucky streak of back-to-back temp jobs had recently dried up. I wasn't about to move back into Lucy and Tim's, so I shifted my focus back to finding a permanent, full-time job.

A week later, I landed an interview for a non-profit children's organization by Griffith Park called Avalon. To make matters better, my old friend, Piper, called with more promising job news.

Piper was also from my Sunset Strip days. She worked for a management company whose clientele included producers and various actors. Dan, an Executive Producer for the MTV show *Punk'd*, was one of her clients. He needed a new assistant and was interviewing people the following afternoon. Piper set up a 3:00 p.m. meeting, which worked out perfectly. My interview at Avalon was at 1:00 p.m. Most of my job interviews never ran more than an hour tops. That gave me plenty of time to get to MTV in Santa Monica.

I woke the next morning, bright-eyed, bushy-tailed and determined to land one of the two jobs I was interviewing for.

After interviewing with the H.R. department at Avalon, they called in a supervisor to speak with me. By the time I met with a third person, a nice woman named Sue, I was in panic mode. It was 2:15 p.m.

Sue spoke with me for an additional half hour

before offering me the job, which I accepted. I was happy to have a steady job, but I desperately wanted a shot at *Punk'd*. Sue mentioned there was paperwork she wanted me to fill out and told me she would be back in a few minutes. The moment she left the room, I grabbed my cell phone and called Piper.

"Is there anyway you can call Dan and tell him I'm on my way?" I asked.

"Sure, but how far away are you?" Piper asked.

"I'm still in Griffith Park but I'm about to run out the door."

"Holy shit, you're not going to get there for at least an hour."

"Please call him and ask if he can still meet me? Please, please, please!" I begged.

"Okay hold on. I'm going to call him on my other line," she said.

I sat on the phone, anxiously tapping my foot and praying she would get back to me before Sue returned.

"Hey honey, Dan said it was fine. He's going to be there for a few more hours, but get there a.s.a.p.!" she said.

"Thank you so much. I owe you big time! Bye!" I said and hung up.

Sue walked in a few moments later with paperwork and told me I would make $17 an hour. It was the most money I had ever made at a job.

"Sue, I hate to be rude but I had a doctor's appointment at 3:00 p.m. in Santa Monica that I'm late for. They can still take me in if I leave now," I said, lying through my teeth.

"Oh my! I'm so sorry we made you late. Don't worry about all this paperwork, you can fill it out on Monday."

I thanked her profusely, then ran out the front door and high tailed it to Santa Monica. The longer I sat in traffic, the angrier I became about possibly blowing my chance at working on the show. I made a decision that I was going to get that job, and I didn't care if I had to beat Dan into giving it to me.

I was sweating profusely as my car raced into the MTV parking lot and doused myself in perfume before getting out of the car. I jogged into the building and fanned myself with my resume on the elevator ride up. When I walked into the main office, I saw a few empty cubicles off to the left. No one was around. I noticed an office in front of me with its door open. A bald gentleman in a white shirt was sitting at his desk, yelling at someone on the phone. He looked to be in his mid 40's. He hung up with whomever he was arguing with, so I poked my head in and smiled.

"You Marisa?" the man asked sternly.

"Yes I am. Are you Dan?" I asked.

"Damn right I am and why the fuck are you so late?" he asked, loudly.

I froze and didn't know what to say. Dan burst out laughing.

"I'm kidding, have a seat. Actually, I'm not kidding. I do want to know why you're so damn late but have a seat anyway," he said.

I sat down on his black leather couch, apologized for my tardiness and blamed it on bad Los Angeles traffic.

My interview with Dan was the complete opposite of what I experienced at Avalon. He cracked a bunch of jokes and told me about the show. He also mentioned he didn't need a brain surgeon to be his assistant, just someone halfway competent that could keep him organized. I suppose I should have been slightly insulted, but I thought it was funny. I was also in no position to point fingers on professionalism, considering how late I was. And not a little late, I was over an hour late. It was inexcusable. If I were Dan, I wouldn't have hired me. I did the only thing I could do. I told him I was a hard worker who was willing to work whatever hours he needed, and I would never be late again.

"Okay last minute Louie, you got the job. Come in at 9:00 a.m. on Monday. Your cubicle is the one right outside my office."

"Thank you so much! I promise I won't disappoint you," I said, smiling.

When I came home, I sat on my bed and thought about the decision I needed to make. I accepted two job offers and now I had to pick one.

The more exciting job was clearly *Punk'd*, but they paid less than Avalon. I wouldn't have health insurance or job stability, which Avalon also offered. Essentially, I would work on *Punk'd* for a few months until filming concluded. Then I would be out of a job for a few more months until the next season started up, provided there would be another season and if Dan brought me back.

The mature decision was to take the job at Avalon. But it was the typical 9-5-desk job, clocking in and out for lunch. It was safe and unchallenging. That wasn't me. I had worked that type of job for the last nine years, and I was certain those jobs would exist in my future.

I wanted to be a writer since I was in grade school. I knew that working on *Punk'd* was the opportunity I needed to get my foot in the door of the entertainment industry, so I made the irresponsible decision to rescind my job offer from Avalon.

I quickly settled into my new job at *Punk'd*. It was the first job I had where I looked forward to going to work everyday. I did standard secretarial duties for Dan and helped the office staff when they needed an extra hand. This was at the height of when Ashton Kutcher and Demi Moore started dating, so it was common to see paparazzi sniffing around the MTV parking lot. They were constantly in the tabloids with the most ridiculous headlines. But when I saw them in the office they were always friendly. They would say "hello" and smile at me when they strolled by my cubicle and were very affectionate with each other. I thought was sweet. It made me wish I had someone to nuzzle up to.

A few weeks later, I went to have drinks with Piper and give her an update on the new job. Unfortunately, neither of us had anything to report on in terms of our relationship status. We both were still painfully single.

"At least you have Ashton to stare at everyday. It's not that bad," Piper said.

"Meh. He's not my type and besides, he's basically my boss. The only guy I'm day dreaming about is Owen Michaels," I replied.

"Owen Michaels?" she asked.

"Yeah, he plays a cop on that Fox show *Bridgepoint.*"

"I had no idea you had a crush on Owen. I totally know him."

"Shut the fuck up!" I yelled.

"Yeah, he's one of our clients."

"What's he like? I saw him at a party a few weeks ago, but I didn't get a chance to go up to him."

"Why don't I let you find out for yourself? I'm going to give him your number. Maybe you guys can get together for a date or something?" she said, casually.

I raised my eyebrow and stared at her.

"What's wrong?" she asked.

"You're out of your damn mind. Why in the hell would Owen Michaels ever agree to go on a blind date? He's used to dating supermodels," I said.

"Exactly for that reason. He's a charming guy

who's used to dating supermodels. He probably wants to date a normal girl for once."

"I'm going to pretend that was a compliment." I said, dryly.

"No seriously. He has a great sense of humor like yours. I think you guys would get along great. He's coming to the office for a meeting tomorrow, so I'll talk to him and give him your number."

"Okay Piper, what ever you say," I said, rolling my eyes.

Piper wasn't one to pull pranks, but things like that don't just happen. You don't daydream about a celebrity, only to have one of your closest friends serve them up on a silver platter. I thought the whole thing was ridiculous, but I went along with her anyway.

The following day at work was a long one, due to extensive prepping for an upcoming shoot. I left the office just in time to sit in rush hour traffic on Santa Monica Blvd. My breaks were screeching and the idling was making my car overheat. I was watching the needle in my temperature gauge slowly rise to "H" when Piper called.

"Hey Piper, my car is about to explode. Can I call you back in a little bit?" I asked, casually.

"Listen, I spoke with Owen and told him all about you. I gave him your number and he said he's definitely going to call you!" she said with excitement.

I still didn't believe her.

"Oh awesome," I said, unenthusiastically.

"Marisa, did you hear what I said?"

"I heard you. I'll believe it when I see it," I said, casually.

I hung up with Piper and thought about what she told me. I didn't understand why she was filling my head with nonsense about Owen. I hadn't dated anyone since Tyler, and I couldn't imagine rebounding with Owen Michaels.

I was driving home from work the following day when my car started to overheat again. I was sitting in Sunset Boulevard traffic, desperately looking for a place to pull over. My phone rang. I didn't recognize the number and assumed it was someone at work in regards to an upcoming shoot.

"Hello?" I asked.

"Marisa?" a male voice asked.

"Yeah. Who's this?"

"Hey, it's Owen Michaels. Piper gave me your number."

I dropped my cell phone and quickly scrambled to pick it back up.

"Hey Owen, sorry about that. I'm driving right now and lost control of my phone," I said, trying to sound calm.

"No worries, so how are ya?"

"I'm good. How are you?"

"I'm great. So you're a friend of Piper's?"

"Yeah, I've known her for quite a few years."

"Awesome. So hey, I'm about to head out but I wanted to see if you'd like to grab dinner tomorrow night?"

I started slapping the passenger's seat with excitement.

"Sure, that sounds great," I said, calmly.

"Cool. I'm staying at the Mondrian on Sunset. Did you want to meet here and we can pick a place to eat when you arrive?"

"Yeah, I can go there," I replied.

"Great. I'll give you a ring tomorrow afternoon darling and we'll make a game plan."

"Sounds good. I'll talk to you tomorrow."

I frantically pushed buttons on my phone to save Owen's number. I gave it the appropriate ringtone of "hallelujah" so I would immediately know anytime he called. Then I promptly called Pandora and proceeded to scream my head off.

"Hey chicky, what's happening?" Pandora asked.

"Oh my god!" I yelled.

"What happened? Are you okay?"

"Omigod…omigod…OH MY GOD!"

"Would you stop saying 'oh my god' and tell me what the fuck happened?"

"OwenMichaelsjustcalledandwe'regoingonadatet omorrownight!" I said as if it were one word.

"SHUT THE FUCK UP!" Pandora yelled.

"I know! Oh my god!"

My dashboard began to beep. The needle on my temperature gauge was dangerously close "H".

"What's that beeping?" she asked.

"Oh it's nothing, just my car overheating," I said, casually.

"So how did all this happen?"

"Well, it's been leaking coolant fluid lately…"

"No, no, no! Not your stupid car! The date with Owen!"

"Oh! He's a client of Piper's. She told me she was going to give him my number, but I thought she was joking."

The beeping continued from my dashboard.

"Shit. I have to pull over somewhere before my car explodes. Let me call you back in a little bit," I told her and promptly hung up.

I was up half the night trying to pick out an outfit to wear on my date with Owen. I didn't want to wear a dress and heels because I didn't want to look like a desperate hooch. This was going to be casual drinks. I finally settled on a pair of slacks with a blouse and some boots.

I was asleep for about an hour or so when I woke up to the scent of grilled hamburgers. I was a bit foggy and thought I was dreaming that Owen and I were on a date at a barbecue. That's when the blast of

Guns N' Roses, "Welcome to the Jungle" scared me out of my comfy slumber.

I looked at my clock. It was almost 4:00 a.m. I got out of bed and angrily threw open the screen door to my balcony. I leaned over and saw my neighbor, Chris, down below. He was flipping burgers and hot dogs on a barbecue, while people sat around in lawn chairs like it was a leisurely, Saturday afternoon.

"Chris...CHRIS!" I yelled over the loud music.

"Hey Marisa, how's it going?" Chris asked, casually.

"Are you crazy? People have to work tomorrow!"

"It's a special occasion though. It's my friend's birthday and we're..."

"I don't give a shit if Axl Rose is sitting in your living room singing karaoke!"

"Listen honey, chill the fuck out..."

"No you listen HONEY! The date of my life is tonight and if I wake up with bags under my eyes, I'm going to take that barbecue and shove it up your ass!" I yelled.

Chris stared at me for a few moments and said, "Okay, we'll turn it down."

I woke the next morning a little tired but sans bags. It was a beautiful day. The sun was shining, the layer of smog wasn't as thick as it usually was, and at the end of the day I was going on a date with my dream man!

Owen called me that afternoon and told about an English pub on Sunset. I was fine with that idea until he mentioned something about me picking him up at his hotel.

The last thing I wanted was for him to get into my piece of shit car. It was barely holding itself together with Scotch tape and paperclips, figuratively speaking. I suggested we go somewhere within walking distance from his hotel. He mentioned Saddleranch across the street. I quickly agreed.

I left work a little early so I would have enough time to prepare for my date. Everything had to be perfect.

I pulled out of my driveway to meet Owen, and the reality finally hit me. I was petrified instead of excited and called Pandora for backup.

"Hey chicky, are you on your way to Owen's hotel?" she asked.

"Yes, but I'm scared. What if he prefers blondes? And now that I look at my outfit, I think I might be underdressed. Should I go home and change?"

"Honey! Listen to me. You're going at 100 right now, slow it down okay? Take a deep breath," she said, calmly.

"I don't feel sexy at all with these pants on. I probably look like a lumberjack. I should have just worn a dress."

"I'm sure you look great. Why don't you put some sexy music on? It'll give you a little boost of confidence. What are you listening to right now?" she asked.

"Um, Journey?"

"Would you turn that horrible shit off? What else do you have?"

"How about Britney?"

"What Britney?"

"I'm a Slave?"

"Ooh, good one put it in!"

I popped a Britney Spears CD into my car stereo and the music started to blast through my speakers.

"Okay, now start dancing sexy," she said.

"What?"

"Start dancing sexy," she reiterated.

"But, I'm in my car trying to drive…"

"I didn't say bust out a piece of cardboard and

do backspins, just move a little!"

I started to move my shoulders back and forth to the beat. Then I started to sing. Pandora joined in on the vocals, and I noticed a person in the car next to me start laughing. I didn't care. I was into the vibe of the song and starting to feel confident. That quickly changed when I pulled up to valet at the Mondrian, and my screeching brakes brought me back to reality.

I got out of my car, grabbed a ticket from the valet and watched my ghetto car screech off into the distance.

The lobby of the Mondrian was gold with white furniture and had hardwood floors. I took a seat and called Owen to let him know I was there.

"Hey Marisa. I just need to brush my teeth but I don't want you to sit in the lobby by yourself. Come up to my room, its room 1014," he said.

"Okay sure," I said, trying to sound calm. "I'll be up in a second."

I walked to the elevators and couldn't find a button to call them. I took a few steps back, looked around the frames and the entire wall of where both elevators stood, yet I couldn't find a button anywhere. I thought maybe it was sensor activated, so I waved my arms around by both elevators. I caught a few people looking at me strangely, so I tried to play it off like I was swatting away a bug.

I took a stroll through the lobby to get a better look at the wall, thinking maybe I missed something. That's when I noticed a lone, wooden stick coming out of the floor. It was about eight feet away from the elevators and had one, silver button. I pushed it. One of the elevators opened. I rolled my eyes and walked in.

The elevator doors opened on the 10th floor. I walked out of the elevator and looked down the long hallway. I started to walk slowly. Questions of doubt ran through my head again, and then I thought of

Britney.

"I'm a Slave For You" popped into my head and the pace of my footsteps picked up to the beat. I felt like John Travolta in the opening scene to *Saturday Night Fever.*

The music in my head and the strutting came to an abrupt halt when the numbers "1014" appeared on a door in front of me. The door was slightly ajar. I gently knocked twice, which caused the door to open a little more. I gasped and tore my hand back.

"Marisa? Is that you?" A man's voice yelled from inside the room.

"Yeah it's me!" I yelled back.

"Come on in!"

"Oh my god…" I mumbled quietly to myself.

I walked in and gently closed the door behind me. Owen was nowhere to be found, but I heard sounds coming from the bathroom. Everything was white. White couches, white bed, white carpet. Two of the four walls of his room were made of glass that showed a spectacular view of the city.

Then it happened in what felt like slow motion. Owen walked out of the bathroom. He was wearing blue jeans, sneakers and an army-green t-shirt with little tears near his shoulders. He smiled as he walked toward me and greeted me with a hug and a kiss on the cheek.

"Hey, it's nice to finally meet you," he said.

"It's nice to meet you too," I said, smiling.

He grabbed a jacket and we made small talk as we walked across the street to Saddleranch. He mentioned he just bought a house in the Hollywood Hills. Construction wasn't completed, so he was staying at the Mondrian for the time being.

A hostess seated us at a table outside as he told me about a script he was working on. I don't remember what it was about. I wasn't paying attention. I was busy staring into his big, green eyes. My gaze was broken when a waitress walked up and took our drink orders. I was about to ask him something about his house when we were interrupted again. This time, it was by two fans sitting at a table next to us.

"Hey you're Owen Michaels!" one guy said.

Owen turned around and smiled.

"Love your show man," another guy said.

"Thanks guys, I really appreciate it," Owen said thoughtfully.

The fans asked him a few things about *Bridgepoint*. Owen answered politely and transitioned his attention back to our date as the waitress dropped off our drinks. She took our dinner orders and skipped off again.

We talked about our families and he asked what I did for a living. When I mentioned I worked on *Punk'd*, he said he knew Dax, one of the actors on the show.

We finished our first round of drinks rather quickly, so we ordered another. I suddenly felt comfortable around Owen. I'm sure part of it was the alcohol, but in all honesty, Owen was a down-to-earth person. He didn't have any hint of an ego. He was actually a nerd. He loved cheesy love songs from artists like Barry Manilow and the Carpenters. He was also a fan of Hair Metal music, which kicked off an hour-long conversation about the Sunset Strip. By the third round of drinks we were singing "Come Sail Away" by Styx rather loudly and didn't care. I didn't see him as Owen Michaels, the star on *Bridgepoint*. He was just a goofy guy named Owen that I was having a fun blind date with. I was finally getting comfortable with him, maybe a little too comfortable.

"I have to ask you something," I said.

"Sure, what's up?" he asked.

"Why did you agree to go out with me?"

He looked confused. I was worried I may have been too bold, so I buried myself in my cocktail.

"Well, why wouldn't I?" he asked.

"You don't even know me and I doubt you have a hard time finding a date," I replied.

"Piper said you were cool, so I didn't think it was a big deal."

"It's kind of funny how that all came about actually."

"Oh really? What happened?"

That's when I quickly sobered up. Those damn drinks and my big mouth were a dangerous combination. I couldn't believe I almost told Owen he was my celebrity crush for the last two years. I might as well have presented him with a pot of boiling water and a rabbit as his housewarming gift. I had to backtrack quickly.

"Uhh...I can't remember exactly how your name came up. But she thought we would get along great and mentioned she was going to chat with you about it," I said, casually.

Luckily for me, he bought my bullshit story.

After finishing our current round of drinks, he asked if I wanted to go back to his room "to hang out".

I knew exactly what that meant. I had always been the good girl though. I never had a one-night stand before. My sexual history consisted of back-to-back boyfriends. But I figured to hell with it. If all it was going to be were a one-night stand, it would be a hell of a first.

We went back to Owen's hotel and created a playlist of cheesy songs on his laptop. We had our own karaoke party in the middle of his hotel room. We sang songs like, "Superstar" from the Carpenters, and "Home Sweet Home" from Mötley Crüe. It was ridiculous and fun. We sang for hours, and then had sex before passing out.

I woke up the next morning with a mild hangover. I knew I looked like shit. Owen was asleep, so I snuck out of bed and tiptoed to the bathroom to make myself presentable. Owen woke up a few minutes later and we talked about how much fun we had the night before. While I got dressed, he grabbed his wallet and pulled out two twenty-dollar bills. I raised an eyebrow and looked at him. He started laughing.

"Oh stop. I'm giving you money for parking. Valet is expensive. I don't want you paying for it," he said.

"Oh thanks," I said, feeling embarrassed.

I gathered my things and told him I had to leave for a lunch date, which was a lie. I knew he had things to do that day, and I didn't want to be a bother. We exchanged a kiss and he told me the words no girl wants to hear after putting out on a first date.

"I had a lot of fun last night, I'll call you tomorrow," he said.

I wanted to cringe but kept a smile on my face. We said our goodbyes, and I called Pandora when I got home.

"Good afternoon Mrs. Michaels," Pandora said.

"Oh shut up," I said, laughing.

"Did you just get home from doing the walk of shame?"

"I prefer to call it a victory lap."

"No way! Did you sleep with him?"

"Of course I did. I'm a big whore," I said, casually.

"That's awesome! I want all the details!"

I was about to fill her in when a call came in on my other line.

"Oh my god, Owen is calling me right now," I said.

"Shut the fuck up! Call me later!" she replied and hung up.

Owen wanted to make sure I got home okay and that I had enough money to pay for parking. I told him everything was fine. He also mentioned he would be back in two weeks once construction on his house was completed. He wanted us to grab dinner again. When we got off the phone I called Pandora back and we both started screaming when I told her the news.

Owen and I kept in touch while he went back to film *Bridgepoint* in Canada. And as promised, we met up when he came back into town a few weeks later. We went to dinner and caught a showing of *Bad Boys 2* at Mann's Chinese Theatre. After the movie, he took me to his new house at the top of Lookout Mountain in the Hollywood Hills.

Owen's house was a three-level home with a den on the bottom floor, which he transformed into a video arcade and movie theatre.

On the main level, along with his kitchen and living room was a guest bedroom and his personal office. Upstairs was his humongous bedroom and large adjoining balcony with a view overlooking the city. His personal bathroom was the size of my living room, and its shower could fit a party of five. He had a beautiful garden in the backyard with a pool and Jacuzzi set in the center. The entire house had hardwood floors and smelled like lavender. It was lovely.

Our second date felt like déjà vu from weeks earlier. Only this time, Owen had a professional karaoke machine in his den. We played with it for hours. He would put on performances like he was singing to an arena. It was hysterical. We were tone deaf but it didn't matter. We caterwauled until the early morning hours, then made our way up to his bedroom and passed out.

I woke the next morning to the sounds of my growling stomach. Owen was beside me, snoring like a wild boar. I decided to sneak downstairs and grab a few snacks to quiet my rumbling tummy.

I put my socks on when I got out of bed and began slipping and sliding due to his smooth, hardwood floors. I took my socks off and tiptoed downstairs to the kitchen. After some careful rummaging, I found some cheese and crackers. It was terribly dark in the living room. I wanted to enjoy the beautiful day outside on the balcony of his bedroom, so I took my snacks upstairs.

I tiptoed into Owen's bedroom. He was still rattling the walls with his snoring. I quietly unlocked the patio doors, and when I opened one of them the house alarm went off. Owen immediately sat up and became tangled in his sheets as he fell out of bed. He was finally able to get up and fumbled for an alarm pad at the door of his bedroom.

"I'm sorry! I didn't know you had an alarm. Do you want some cheese and crackers?" I said smiling as I raised the tray of food towards him.

Once he turned the alarm off, he chuckled a few times and joined me out on the patio.

Owen and I got together a few more times during his visits home from filming in Canada. But as the weeks passed, I noticed his calls became fewer and far between.

The downfall of my relationship with Owen started the day he showed up at my apartment, completely unannounced. It wasn't like him. He always called me ahead of time when he knew he was coming to town.

I was coming home from an early dinner with Piper when he called. He was in my neighborhood after a busy day of meetings and wanted to have a mellow night in.

"Should I just go to your place in about an hour or so?" I asked.

"I'm actually right around the corner from your apartment. My friend is going to drop me off if that's cool?"

It wasn't cool. I was a hot sweaty mess from a

long day's work. I also hadn't washed my hair or shaved my legs in three days. I needed time to shower and get ready.

"Um yeah that's cool. I'll see you in a few minutes then," I said, uncomfortably.

I parked my car and barreled up the stairs of my apartment building and swung open the front door. I took a glance at the living room. It was passable, so I ran into my bedroom. There were clothes and papers all over my bed. Anything that wasn't in its proper place got thrown in the hamper, and I sprayed my bedroom with raspberry body spray.

I ran into my bathroom. Anything on the counter was thrown in a tray and tossed under the sink. I was sweating profusely and started to pull my shirt over my head when the doorbell rang.

I grabbed a small towel to wipe down my face and chest. Then I dowsed myself in perfume and ran to the front door to let Owen in. After exchanging a hug and kiss hello, he sat down on my living room couch.

"Sorry I'm a bit sweaty, I just got home," I said. "I'm going to hop in the shower real quick but I'll be right out," I said as walked toward the bathroom.

"Okay, I'll come in with you," he said.

"What?"

"Come on, it'll be fun!"

"You can't," I said.

"Why not?" he asked.

"Well, there's not enough room. It's a tiny shower."

He walked past me and said, "It'll be fine. I don't take up a lot of room."

Owen opened the shower curtain, turned a few nozzles and began to get undressed. I was mortified.

"Owen, I swear I'll be five minutes. Why don't you make yourself a drink and watch TV?" I said, trying to hide my panic.

"What's wrong? Afraid I'll see you naked?" he said with a flirty smile.

"Well, no…"

"Oh stop being silly and just get in," he said and then hopped in the shower.

I looked at my sweaty face in the mirror. I couldn't believe what was happening. It was karma paying me back for breaking the hearts of sweet guys like Dexter and Karl. Owen always saw me perfectly primped. Now, he was about to see me for the hairy wildebeest I was.

I noticed a razor sitting on my bathroom sink. There was nothing I could do about my legs or nether regions, but I could enter the shower without hairy armpits. I grabbed the razor, bit my lip and swiped it twice under each arm. I put the razor down and Owen opened up the shower curtain.

"Hey, what are you doing out there?" he asked.

"Um, nothing. I'm getting undressed," I said, pulling on my pants.

About a half hour later, we were in my bedroom getting dressed when he received a phone call.

"Oh no way…yeah that sounds like fun… I don't have a car though…that would be great, here's the address," he said on the phone.

I had no idea what sounded fun or why he was giving someone my address. He hung up with them a few moments later.

"My friend, Tom, is having a party tonight. He's picking me up right now," he said.

"I thought you were tired and wanted to stay in?" I asked.

"I was, but I haven't seen Tom in a long time. You can come too if you want?"

"I can't. Look at me. My hair is soaking wet, I'm not ready to go out."

"I'm sorry, I didn't know he was going to be in

town. I want to see him while he's here because he leaves next week for Germany and won't be back for months."

"It's fine. Go and have fun. I'm going to stay in."

"Are you sure?" he asked.

Owen's phone rang and he answered.

"Yeah, I'll be right there," he said to the person on the phone and quickly hung up.

"I'm sorry, Tom is about to pull up outside," he said with a regretful smile.

"Just go. Have a good time. I'll talk to you later," I said, diplomatically.

Owen gave me a big kiss before running out the door. As I sat on my bed with a head full of sopping, wet hair, it hit me. I was nothing more to Owen than a booty call.

Over the next few weeks, pictures of Owen were popping up everywhere. He was at movie premieres, fund-raising events and concerts all right in Los Angeles. My phone never rang once.

I called Piper to tell her about my dilemma with Owen. That's when she put everything into perspective over a few glasses of wine and a chicken salad the size of a trough at the Rainbow.

Piper took a sip of her wine and said, "I'm really sorry for setting you up with Owen. I thought you understood what the situation was with him."

"What situation?" I asked.

"Owen is a funny, charming and charismatic guy. He's respectful, but he's also a bit of a player."

"Yeah, I figured that out by now."

"I'm sorry honey," she said, rubbing my hand.

"It's my own fault. What else could I expect after I basically threw my vagina at him on our first date? It's not exactly 'bring her home to mom' behavior."

I couldn't fault Owen, nor was I mad at him. He never once said he loved me or made promises he didn't keep.

After my chat with Piper, I stopped making any effort to talk to Owen. We didn't speak for a few months, and then he started emailing me. Every few weeks he would send me a short email, asking how I was and what I had been up to. When he changed his contact information, I was surprised to be on the small email of people he gave that info to. We had officially entered the "friend zone".

Shortly after Owen and I stopped dating, I had another headache to worry about. Money.

*Punk'd* was nearing the end of its current season That meant I would be out of work for a few months until the next season started filming. I was also waiting on another possible job from Dan. He was working on a TV pilot for Warner Bros and said he might hire me to coordinate the show. So on top of having a mildly bruised heart from Owen, I was severely stressed out over where my next paycheck would come from.

After laying low for a few weeks, Piper called me for a "girl's night" out. Some of her co-workers wanted to check out a Greek restaurant in West Hollywood called Sofi. I wasn't feeling particularly social, but it was a Saturday night. Sulking in a Greek garden with a glass of wine in my hand was better than sitting at home alone.

I went to Piper's that afternoon and we spent the day shopping. When we got back to her place, some girls from her work came over and we grabbed a cab to Sofi's restaurant.

We indulged in copious amounts of appetizers and wine while we cackled the night away. I was pouring myself another glass of wine when a blonde woman seeming to be in her early 30s walked up and took a seat at our table.

"Hey everyone this is Chelsea, one of my clients. Chelsea this is everyone," Piper said.

The cackling resumed after introducing ourselves to Chelsea, and I leaned over to Piper.

"Have I met her before? She looks familiar," I whispered.

"You probably met her at some of the industry parties we've gone to. That's Chelsea Handler. She's on a show called *Girls Behaving Badly*," Piper whispered back.

"Oh, okay. I've heard of the show, but I've never seen it before."

"It's a hidden camera show with an all girl cast. Dan loves her and thinks she's too talented to be on that show. I have to agree. She's really funny, she just hasn't gotten her big break yet."

Funny was an understatement. Chelsea was obnoxious and a smartass. I knew we would get along famously.

After another round of drinks, Piper mentioned there was an industry party nearby. She wasn't sure if she was on the guest list but suggested we go there anyway.

We finished up at Sofi's, and I hopped into Chelsea's car with Piper, while the rest of the girls cabbed it to the party. On the way there, I said we should have a backup plan in case we weren't on the list.

"If we're not on the list, we'll just say you're that singer, Michelle Branch," Chelsea said.

"You're crazy, I don't look anything like her," I said, laughing.

"Brown hair, brown eyes. It all looks the same," she said as she got out of her car.

I can't recall what club the party was at. It didn't matter anyway. The doorman told us in his snooty tone that we weren't on his list.

"Do you know that she's Michelle Branch? The famous singer?" Chelsea said sarcastically to doorman as she pointed at me.

I started laughing, grabbed Chelsea's hand and said, "Come on, lets go."

We walked away, and I asked the girls what they wanted to do. Some of the girls were feeling lazy. Piper wasn't feeling peppy either. She suggested we go back to her house and have a few more drinks.

"That's not very fun. I want to go to another bar," I said.

"Yeah me too," Chelsea said.

Chelsea raised an eyebrow at me. I responded by raising an eyebrow back at her. We said our goodbyes to the girls, and I followed Chelsea back to her car.

We talked about where to go and she mentioned a bar in Hollywood called Jones. It was down the street on Santa Monica near La Brea. She knew one of the bartenders there who always gave her free drinks. My employment status was still up in the air, so complimentary drinks sounded right in my price range.

We walked into Jones and lucky for us, the bartender that Chelsea knew was working that night. He gave us ridiculously strong drinks and set us up with a booth.

Chelsea and I were gabbing and sipping on our cocktails when two smarmy-looking guys approached us. Each was standing at either end of our booth, waiting for us to move over so they could sit down. I didn't budge and neither did Chelsea. Sensing she was as uninterested by those two as I was, I decided to mess with them.

One of them asked what we did for a living. I said Chelsea and I were partners in a midget tossing business. She smirked and took a sip of her drink.

Those guys weren't stupid. They were annoying, but not stupid. They knew I was full of shit, so they started asking questions about the business, assuming Chelsea or I would get tripped up. But if one of us didn't know the answer to a question, we tossed it to the other. Miraculously, we ran a smooth tennis match of bullshit between those two morons.

"Come on, nobody runs a midget tossing business. You guys are bullshitting us," one of the guys said.

"No, honestly. We were at a Midget Expo earlier today in Santa Monica picking out new talent," Chelsea said, casually.

"Oh really? Well how do you decide what to charge for each midget? Huh?" one of the guys asked.

"Well...that's more of a Marisa question. She handles the financial details of the business," Chelsea said, tossing the ball back in my court, figuratively speaking.

"We charge by the pound," I said, dryly.

Chelsea bit her lip and dove into her drink to keep from laughing.

At that point, the guys had enough of us and told us to enjoy our night. Chelsea and I burst out laughing when they walked away.

"I've never seen anyone who wasn't an actress adlib like that and keep a straight face before. That was awesome!" Chelsea said.

"I thought I was going to crack on that last one," I said, laughing.

We talked about the entertainment business and the wild world of dating men. I left my dalliance with Owen out of the conversation. I knew Hollywood was a small town. There was a chance she might know him, or worse, have dirt on him I wouldn't want to hear.

We finished our 2nd round of drinks as last call was yelled out. On the way back to my place, she mentioned her birthday was coming up the following weekend. She was thinking of having a party at her place and told me I should go. I gave her my number and told her to call me when she figured out her plans.

A few days later, Piper called. She said Chelsea had a falling out with management and was no longer a client. Unfortunately, my invitation to her birthday party got caught in the crossfire. I never heard from Chelsea again.

Shortly after meeting Chelsea, I started thinking about my circle of friends and how I made amends with Dina. If Dina and I could move past everything, hopefully Cassidy could too.

A few weeks later, I went to a Halloween party thrown by Amie and her husband. I knew Dina and Pixie would be there too, so I threw on a costume and drove myself to the Valley. I walked onto the patio that was reserved for the party when I ran into Amie. She greeted me with a big hug.

"I'm so glad you made it! Pixie just got here too. She's somewhere around here. Oh and Dina and Cassidy are at the bar," she said before skipping off to greet another newcomer.

I wasn't expecting Cassidy to be there. It was the opportunity I wanted for the last several years. I made my way toward the bar and was thinking about what I would say to her when she came up from behind.

"Hey, how's it going?" she asked, smiling.

"I'm great, how are you?" I replied.

"Pretty good, a little jetlagged from my flight."

"So you're still living in New York?" I asked.

"Yeah, but I want to move back to L.A."

I was about to apologize to her for all the past ridiculousness when Dina and Pixie interrupted us. The four of us walked over to the bar and ordered some drinks. We were cackling within moments and it felt like old times.

I never got the chance to sit down and have a heart-to-heart with Cassidy that night. But we did exchange numbers and kept in touch when she went back to New York.

Cassidy moved back to Los Angeles a short time later. Although we rekindled our friendship, we hadn't addressed our initial falling out. But I felt we were at a place in our friendship where I could bring it up. We met at our old stomping grounds, El Compadre, and spoke candidly about what happened between us all those years ago.

It turns out she was never bothered by my feelings for Dresden. She didn't love him and would have been fine with us dating. Her issue was that I hid everything from her, and she was right. If I had come clean from day one our fallout probably wouldn't have happened.

"You do know that we found out through Kennedy right?" she asked.

"What are you talking about?" I replied.

"Dina, Amie and I were at my house and we suspected something was going on. Kennedy showed up and we had her call you and ask you questions about Dresden while we listened on the other line. That's how we found out."

"Are you kidding me?" I said.

"You didn't know?"

"Of course I didn't know. I had no idea until right now."

"Oh yeah, she totally played both sides of the fence."

"She said the reason you were mad at me was because people told you he and I were having sex at your house," I said.

"Nope. I've never heard that rumor before. She probably made that up as a reason to explain why I was suddenly mad at you. I was pissed after I heard that phone call and that's why I stopped talking to you."

"What a bitch! I can't believe she set me up like that."

I hadn't seen Kennedy in years, and I truly was

blown away that she did that to me. She and Cassidy were my closest friends back then. I trusted them with my life. I thought about calling Kennedy to give her a piece of my mind, but didn't.

If I could, I would have handled the Dresden/Cassidy situation differently and been honest from the beginning. Cassidy made light of it by saying we were young and stupid. She was right. It was so long ago. I felt silly at the thought of calling Kennedy out. Sure, she was wrong for what she did. But I was wrong too and Cassidy owned up to certain things too. We laughed it off and finished our dinner with a second round of margaritas.

After making peace with Cassidy, I had another blast from the past pop back into my life. None other than my old friends from Blackboard Jungle, no pun intended.

Blackboard Jungle was one of many bands that played on the Sunset Strip during the hair band days of the '80s and early '90s. I recently heard rumors about a reunion show, and it was finally confirmed for the Whisky in the first week of June.

Blackboard Jungle hadn't played together in about six or seven years. I wasn't about to miss that show and neither was Spencer.

When we arrived at the Whisky, I wasn't prepared for what I saw. I stayed in touch with many people from my Sunset Strip days, but this was more like a rock-and-roll high school reunion of yesteryear. I couldn't believe how many people came out of the woodwork for that show. I hadn't seen most of them in well over a decade, many when I still had a mouth full of braces. Now, we were older and a few were a little heavier. Some had ditched the long hair and makeup, while others looked like they never left the 80s.

Spencer and I made our way through the crowd

and stood in the front row. It was strange being against that stage again. For the first time, I felt old. The last time I stood there, I was in a completely different headspace. I was a carefree teenager. But as I looked around at people on their cell phones, posting on social media, I suddenly felt grateful. I was grateful to be older, hopefully a little wiser, but most of all happy that I had a childhood without the intrusion of the Internet or Social Media.

Blackboard Jungle took the stage, and it took me back to the good ole days of the Burbank house. I thought about all the fun times there with the guys, Kennedy and Ramie, and how I used to follow Brent from Faster Pussycat around like a lovesick puppy.

The night was filled with numerous hugs and recalling many of our Sunset Strip memories. At some point in the evening, two female acquaintances of mine had a little too much to drink and brawled in front of the Whisky. That didn't surprise me. It wouldn't be our sick and twisted Hollywood family if there weren't a mishap.

It was great seeing all of my old friends again, but it was also a slap of reality. Everyone had moved on, gotten married and some even had kids. I normally wouldn't have thought about it so much, but my dreaded 30$^{th}$ birthday was around the corner.

When I was in high school, I thought I would be married, own a house and maybe have a kid by the time I was 30. My reality was that I was sharing an apartment the size of a shoebox, I had a job in an industry that offered no job security, and I was single with no boyfriend potential as far as the eye could see. I was clearly in no mood to celebrate. But after some mild nudging from a few girlfriends, I agreed to meet up for cocktails the weekend before my birthday.

On the evening of my actual birthday, I was watching TV in my bedroom. I had a glass of red wine in one hand and a plate of cheese bites in the other. I looked at the clock. It was 11:58 p.m. My heart raced for a few moments, and then a strange moment of calm came over me.

I realized that turning 30 was just a number and nothing more. There were people in the world with real problems and substantial things to be worried about. None of which included the nonsense I was stressing over. I was in good health with a roof over my head and plenty of food to eat. The planets were not going to align and crash into each other, at least not that I knew of.

I looked up to the clock and it read 12:01 a.m. I laughed at how silly I was to make a big deal out of nothing. I had turned 30, but so had millions of other women on the planet. Their world didn't end so why should mine? I raised my glass in the air and took a good hit of wine. Big fucking deal.

I was 30 and fabulous.

# 5

# THE WACKY WORLD OF TELEVISION

*I*n addition to leaving my 20s behind, the winter of 2003 also marked the end of the 2$^{nd}$ season of *Punk'd*. Dan said he would bring me back for the 3$^{rd}$ season, but that wouldn't start prepping for another month or so.

Dan also came through by giving me an opportunity to move up the career ladder. He hired me as a Production Coordinator for his Warner Bros TV pilot called *Brainiac*.

I had never coordinated a show before, but I shadowed the coordinators on *Punk'd* for the last few months. I was confident I could handle the job. I was also fortunate to have an amazing Production Manager by the name of Deb. She was patient and more than willing to show me the Coordinator ropes of a running a shoot.

While I worked on *Brainiac* there were several shows in the works for the *Punk'd* crew during its hiatus. In addition to *Brainiac*, Dan was also prepping for another pilot called *Granted*. It was for MTV and starred Frankie Muniz who was on Fox's *Malcolm in the Middle* at the time. The *Brainiac* and *Granted* pilots were polar opposites in terms of their premise. *Brainiac* was originally a British based show. Dan wanted to produce the American version, which was a humorous take on testing modern day myths. *Granted* was more of a *Make a Wish Foundation* concept with Frankie Muniz acting as the host and fairy godmother, so to speak. I was hoping to work on both shows. Unfortunately, the filming schedules overlapped.

The 3rd season of *Punk'd* started shortly after I finished on *Brainiac*. After five, grueling weeks of getting my Coordinator ass kicked, I found myself back at the *Punk'd* offices, sitting at my old desk.

There was a crew meeting with Ashton during my first week back at *Punk'd*. He told us things would be different with the new season.

First, it was getting harder to "punk" celebrities. Everyone was paranoid. There were numerous reports of faux *Punk'd* happenings all over Los Angeles. Anytime there was a celebrity mishap, they were convinced it was us. Celebrities warned their other celebrity friends, that there would be hell to pay if they set them up for a prank.

To throw everyone off the scent, Ashton sent out a news release that *Punk'd* wasn't coming back for another season. If anyone asked what show we worked on, we were instructed to say an MTV show called *Snafu*. The *Punk'd* logo wouldn't appear on Call Sheets or any other documentation related to the show.

Another concern in doing those bits was being able to air them. Usually, the setup and execution was the hardest part. But the final step in cementing a successful prank was getting the celebrity to sign off on a release. Most were good sports about it. Others needed some mild persuasion. Then there were celebrities like baseball player, Alex "A-Rod" Rodriguez who refused to sign. I wasn't on set for A-Rod's prank. But word around the office was that he "allegedly" badmouthed some fellow baseball colleagues during his prank, and that was why he didn't want his episode to air.

Working on the 3rd season of *Punk'd/Snafu* was more fun than the previous season. They made me a dinner patron in two different pranks. One skit involved basketball player, Carmelo Anthony, and another with model, Tyra Banks.

Neither of Dan's pilots was picked up to go to series, which threw a wrench in my future employment status. I planned to work on one of his shows when *Punkd/Snafu* wrapped, and it was coming up fast. I was telling my dire straights to an MTV producer named Anna, when she mentioned she could use an extra hand with an upcoming show.

I assumed it was another MTV pilot. When she told me it was *The 2004 MTV Movie Awards,* I nearly shit myself. On the list to perform were artists like Eminem and the Beastie Boys, which had me squealing like a lovesick teenager.

The show was filming on a soundstage at Sony Pictures Studios in Culver City. Lindsey Lohan was scheduled to be the host. This was back when she was a sweet, little redhead that dated Wilmer Valderrama. My job was to look after a smaller soundstage where Lindsey would be rehearsing her opening number and to assist Anna when needed.

Anna brought me on a few days before the show. She gave me a tour of the dressing rooms and various stages we would utilize, and then left me at stage 28, the stage I would be in charge of. She also introduced me to an Associate Producer named Jill who would become a huge pain in my ass. From what I was told, Jill didn't have much production experience. She was only hired because she had a relative who worked at MTV.

Shortly after Anna left me at stage 28, a choreographer by the name of Shane Sparks strolled in with a few of his dancers. He gave me a CD of the music they would be dancing to and asked if I could run the boom box during rehearsal. I wasn't doing anything but warming my seat at the moment, so I agreed to help out.

Various crewmembers strolled in and out of the stage during the dancer's rehearsal. About an hour later, Lindsey walked in with Wilmer. They were both friendly. He took a seat next to me at a small foldout table while she went to meet Shane and the rest of the dancers. Anna came in a short time later to see how Lindsey was getting acclimated. She felt uncomfortable with strangers popping in and out of the stage while she rehearsed. She only wanted people on the soundstage that absolutely needed to be there. Anna said she would set up a few Production Assistants (PAs) outside to keep people from wandering onto the stage during her rehearsals.

I felt I didn't need to be there either. Wilmer could work the boom box in my absence. But when I stood up to leave, Lindsey told me to could stay. I watched her rehearsal and Shane tweaked some of the choreography to her liking.

The first few days of prepping for the show were uneventful. I spent most of it sitting in on Lindsey's rehearsals and running around like a hamster to help Anna. I also spent a few hours here and there keeping Jill off my stage. She felt she should be allowed to go anywhere including Lindsey's rehearsals, which I always put a stop to.

Jill's sense of entitlement was through the roof. Anna was her direct supervisor, but she didn't listen to her. After a brief chat with Anna about Jill's attitude problem, Anna gave me carte blanche in dealing with all things Jill, which I took full advantage of.

I denied her access to my stage at least a dozen times during those first few days. She was a little star-fucking flea that hopped around the Sony lot, looking for celebrities. Wherever the action was is where she wanted to be. If Lindsey was rehearsing, she wanted to be watching. When other celebrities arrived for rehearsals or run-throughs, she wanted to be in charge. Most of the PAs hated her and rightly so. She didn't care for manual labor and didn't lift a finger when I was stocking the artist trailers or helping the PAs with their duties.

It was early afternoon the day before the show. Lindsey finished rehearsing and everyone broke for lunch. I was walking to the catering tent when I ran into Scout, a Japanese girl I knew from the Sunset Strip days. She had just auditioned and booked the part of a samurai girl for Eminem's performance with D12.

Scout and I were eating lunch together when Anna walked by. Lindsey's rehearsals were almost done for the day, and Anna wanted help with Eminem and D12's rehearsal. They were going to rehearse their new song, "My Band", and she needed someone to wrangle the samurai girls back and forth to the main stage. The time of their rehearsal coincided with Lindsey finishing hers, so I volunteered. I couldn't believe I was going to Eminem and D12's rehearsal!

After we finished lunch, Scout went back to her soundstage to rehearse. I went back to mine and waited for Lindsey and the dancers to return. Things were quiet for about a half hour until a man who claimed to do press for the Beastie Boys walked onto my stage. He wanted to use a small corner of my soundstage to take some press photos for the Beastie Boys. I almost choked on my gum.

"Will there be any props or set up involved?" I asked, trying to control my excitement.

"No set up. The natural light here will be fine. We just want to take a few press photos. I can have everyone out of here in about twenty to thirty minutes tops," he replied.

Lindsey wasn't due back for another hour. I told the guy it was fine. A few minutes later, Ad Rock, Mike D and MCA turned the corner and walked in my direction.

The press manager introduced me to the guys and we all shook hands. While the photo shoot commenced, I stood by with my arms crossed like I was doing something important, when all I wanted to do was tell them I loved them since I was 13. I caught MCA looking at me a few times, but no part of that was lascivious. I knew it was because I was staring at them like a crazed lunatic.

The shoot was done in under a half hour, as promised. I wanted to take a picture with them. Although none of my immediate supervisors were around, I still didn't ask. That was the number one rule. Any crew hassling celebrities or trying to get pictures with them would be fired. I watched the Beastie Boys walk away and ran back to my table to scribble down the brief encounter in my journal.

Lindsey showed up with Wilmer and rehearsed for a few hours. After shutting down my soundstage, I went over to Scout's where she was rehearsing with the rest of the samurai girls. When they finished rehearsal, I escorted them to the main stage. Eminem arrived with D12 a few minutes later. They wore casual clothes, but I was told they were going to dress up like Guns N' Roses for their performance on the show.

I took a seat in the front row and kicked my feet up as I watched Eminem do Axl's infamous worm dance. They ran through the song three times. After escorting the girls back to their soundstage, I helped Anna with a few more things and didn't get home until 2:00 a.m. I was exhausted and had to be back at Sony by 7:30 a.m. that same morning.

After a whopping four hours of sleep, I went back to the Sony stages and met Anna who gave me my credentials for the day. I was given a working 'Crew Pass', which gave me all access. I could walk onto any stage, any room and any backstage area that I wanted. She also gave me a production schedule that showed the order of every presenter, performance and award for the show.

The rest of my morning was chaos and flew by in a flash. By early afternoon, I finally had a moment alone on my soundstage. I was writing in my journal when I overheard on my walkie that Eminem and D12 had arrived. They complained their dressing rooms were too small for their entourage and also wanted rooms with showers. I immediately chimed in.

"Hey guys, this is Marisa on stage 28. I have five empty dressing rooms for Eminem and D12. Two of them have showers if someone wants to escort them over here," I said, trying to contain my excitement.

"Copy that Marisa, we're sending them over," a voice said from the walkie. "Guys! Eminem and D12 are on the move to 28!" they continued.

The dressing rooms were located on the 2$^{nd}$ floor of my stage. A railing outlined the walkway outside the dressing rooms so that guests could safely look down on the soundstage below.

A few minutes later, Eminem walked onto my soundstage with D12. Right behind them was an entourage of people and a friendly but stern guy who introduced himself as Mark. Eminem and D12 didn't acknowledge me, only Mark did. He waved over a huge black guy named Stevion and said he was Eminem's bodyguard. Stevion introduced himself. He was sweet and very friendly, despite his overwhelming stature. Mark kindly thanked me for letting them use the dressing rooms and escorted everyone upstairs.

The guys from D12 came downstairs a short time later, dressed for the show. They were escorted to the main stage while Eminem stayed in his dressing room.

I had one of our PA's hook up a monitor, so I could watch a live feed of the show from my stage. We set it up in the middle of the floor, next some coolers that were filled with snacks for the crew.

I hadn't heard from Anna since she gave me my credentials earlier that morning. I assumed she was tearing her hair out and running around the lot somewhere. With her being busy, I didn't think it would be an issue if I popped onto the main stage to see a few performances. I could care less about the actual show. I wanted to see Eminem and Beastie Boys perform. Nothing was happening on my stage anyway, except for Eminem hanging out in his dressing room with his door closed.

I was watching the live feed of the show when Ashton Kutcher walked onto the main stage. I checked the production schedule Anna gave me earlier. He was about to introduce the Beastie Boys.

There were a few PAs to look after Eminem on my soundstage. I told them I needed to take care of something "important" by the main stage and would be right back.

When I strolled into the backstage area, it was packed with celebrities trying to leave and take their seats. Paris Hilton was there with her then boyfriend, Nick Carter, from Backstreet Boys. I saw Queen Latifah and Snoop Dogg, the latter who reeked of marijuana. Carmen Electra was with Dave Navarro, and Uma Thurman was also there among others.

I didn't want to take a chance at getting in trouble with Anna. I left the backstage area and blended in with the audience near the front of the stage.

The Beastie Boys performed their new single "Ch-Check It Out". I was bouncing up and down but everyone around me was a bunch of deadbeats. I couldn't believe people were just standing around, tapping their feet. When the Beastie Boys finished, I ran back to my soundstage.

I was watching the live feed with a few PAs when I heard the sound of footsteps walking up behind me. I didn't turn around. I thought it was more crewmembers coming in to watch the show. The footsteps became louder and that's when Eminem walked up beside me. He said nothing as he pulled a small cooler closer to the TV and sat down. Mark and Stevion stood right behind him.

Eminem watched the show for about ten minutes and never said a word to any of us. He had a white doo rag on his head, a baggy white sleeveless shirt and baggy black pants. I couldn't believe that one of my favorite new artists was sitting five feet away from me, and I couldn't do a damn thing about it.

Eminem only stayed for a few minutes before going back upstairs to change and leaving with Stevion and Mark to the main stage. I casually strolled out a few minutes later to catch his performance.

Halfway through Eminem's set, the samurai girls came out. All were dressed in kimonos, wielding samurai swords, except for Scout. They put her in a schoolgirl outfit with pigtails and placed her in front of the girls, swinging a mace.

I ran back to my soundstage after Eminem finished and was watching the show when Scout walked in. We jumped up and down, celebrating her performance as if she were Meryl Streep.

Eminem returned to my stage with the guys from D12 and some of their entourage. Proof, one of the guys from D12, took an immediate liking to Scout who was still dressed in her schoolgirl outfit. He chatted her up while more of their entourage made their way onto the soundstage.

Eminem and the D12 guys stayed on the floor, chatting amongst themselves when the Beastie Boys walked in. Eminem was one of my favorite new artists. Beastie Boys were legends that I grew up listening to. To have them congregating together, a few steps away from me was too much.

Everyone left my stage about a half hour later. I called a PA named Mike on my walkie to help me clean the dressing rooms. When Mike arrived on my stage, he was carrying a large paper bag full of clothing and hats.

"Is that trash?" I asked.

"No way," he replied. "I just raided the dressing rooms in the main building," he continued.

"Please tell me you didn't just jack half of the guests on the show."

"No, no it's fine. Celebrities always leave stuff in their rooms. Most of it is given to them for free by sponsors who want them to wear their stuff. They have no problem leaving it behind," he said.

"Are you sure?" I asked.

"Yeah, I always ask Anna for the go ahead. You've never raided the rooms before?"

"I've never worked on an Awards Show before so no, I haven't."

Mike called Anna on his walkie and asked if we could clean out the dressing rooms on my stage. She replied we could and that there was an after party in one of the tents by the main stage when we were finished.

We went through the dressing rooms, but Eminem and D12 didn't leave much behind. I found a new pair of men's Nikes, that I later gave to my brother-in-law. I also picked up one of Eminem's baggy, white sleeveless shirts. It had a 'Shady 8' rubber logo sewn onto the front and fit me like a dress, but I kept it anyway.

It was almost midnight by the time I shut down my soundstage. The 2$^{nd}$ annual Blackboard Jungle reunion show was that night. I knew I was going to have a hectic evening, but a small part of me was hoping I would get out in time to see the show.

Mike and I locked up our goodies in the production office and went to the after party, which was hardly a party. When we arrived most of the people had cleared out and gone to the REAL parties. The bar was still going, so Mike and I grabbed a free drink. We spoke for a few moments until he ran into someone he knew and walked off. I looked around the semi-empty tent. I was bored. My drink was stiff and I was tired. I left the drink on a tabletop and went back to the production office to get my things.

When I got home that night, I barely had the energy to shower. I passed out within moments of landing on my bed and was grateful Anna didn't book me to wrap out the show.

After taking a few well-needed days off, I resumed my job search. I contacted my production friends at MTV and told them I was looking for work. I also spoke with Eden at the March Agency who booked me on most of my temp jobs.

I was out of work for about a week or so when I received a call from Eden. She offered me a 3-week assignment at Silex Development doing administrative work for a manager named Luanne. It was straightforward secretarial duties. Mainly things like answering the phone, filing, and whatever other assistance Luanne needed. The pay was $13 an hour, quite a drop from what I was used to making on shows. But it was more than nothing, so I accepted the job.

Silex was a government agency. My job was the most cookie cutter job I had ever worked in my life. I was given a timecard and told to clock in every morning when I came in and every evening before I left, as well as lunches. I had a cubicle outside Luanne's office, just like the other secretaries with their respective managers.

I was the only temp assistant there. Most of the secretaries took an immediate disliking to me, except for Rocki, the sarcastic African princess.

Rocki was the only woman in my age range, so it made sense that we got along. The rest of the secretaries were a bunch of grumpy, old bags in their 50s and 60s who passed the time by filing their nails until retirement.

Most of the older secretaries at Silex had been there for years, some their whole lives. They were unmotivated and stuck in a rut that is a government job. Mouthing off and being lazy weren't grounds for termination. You had to do something substantial to get fired, and boy did I ruffle some feathers when I started working at Silex.

The problem? I was young and worked hard. That's what pissed off those cranky, old yentas. I was the most productive, young secretary in the office. I made them look bad, and they weren't shy about sharing their feelings toward me either.

Because I was a temp worker, I wasn't allowed to have a security card to get into the office. I had to be buzzed in at the north door entrance by the receptionist, Molly. And good golly, Miss Molly was another old bag that hated me too. Every time she had to buzz me in, she made a sourpuss face like it was such a bother. To avoid her, I started leaving doorstoppers in the south door. It was usually a small book or something of that nature, so I could easily get back in. But once Molly and the other secretaries saw me doing that, they would pull them and lock me out of the office.

The work that took them a day to do, I completed in a few hours. It was an easy workload. My 8-hour workdays usually consisted of about an hour to two hours of solid work. The rest of the time I was looking for things to keep me busy. And because Silex was a government agency, most of the social networking sites were blocked.

Trying to kill six plus hours a day might as well have been twelve. It was a waste of valuable time. I wanted to spend it being productive and that's when I came up with the idea to write a book.

Blackboard Jungle had recently played their 2nd reunion show. Most of my friends who went said it was better than the previous year. The show was becoming a yearly event where people would fly out from all over the country. I felt it was the perfect time to start compiling a book about my years during the Sunset Strip's glam rock era.

The idea sounded exciting but I didn't know where to start. I had written since I was in grade school, but those were short stories and essays. I had never compiled a book before.

I started keeping journals at the age of 12, so that part of my life was well documented. But to make notes for the book, I would have to take on the painstaking chore of reading through those old journals. The problem was that everything during that time period had been written by hand or via typewriter. I couldn't dump a box of journals on my desk at work and start shuffling through the pages. I needed an inconspicuous way to go about it. That's when I remembered the office had a multifunctional copy machine, which doubled as a scanner with Wi-Fi.

All of my early journals were neatly placed into binders. Each day at work, I would sneak into the copy room with a few binders and email myself scanned pages of my journal. It took me three days to get five years worth of journals scanned. The result was five, monster digital files. Each contained a year of my teenage life, which I could casually scroll through on my work computer.

A few days before my assignment at Silex ended, I received a call from Sean, a producer I knew from MTV. He was also a producer for a show called *America's Next Top Model*. They were about to start filming their 4$^{th}$ season and needed an office coordinator right away. He put me in touch with their Line Producer. Within a few days I landed the job.

Although I was excited to work on a hit show, I had never fully coordinated one on my own before. I gained a lot of experience on *Brainiac*, but I also had Deb holding my hand the entire time. I didn't count the *MTV Movie Awards* because I was more of a glorified PA than anything else. When I told Deb I landed the *Top Model* gig she was thrilled and said I could call her with any questions. It was an offer I took her up on.

The production schedule for *America's Next Top Model* was insane. There was no hiatus between seasons and they filmed two seasons a year. While one season went into post-production, they would be prepping for the next. Working in the office was fun, but if I wanted to continue my career in TV production, I had to get more set experience.

There were three producing teams that worked on the show. I recently heard that one of the field coordinators wouldn't be returning for season 5. I jumped at the opportunity to work on set. I spoke with the higher ups on the show and my wish was granted. I would make the switch to field coordinator when I finished wrapping the current season.

I was usually stuck in our main office during most of season 4. But on a few rare occasions when extra help was needed, I would visit the set. During that particular season, the girls lived in a humongous loft in a sketchy part of downtown L.A. The loft was considerably large, so they filmed the eliminations there too. A makeshift production office and control room was built into the garage level, while the girls living quarters and elimination room was on the 2nd floor above.

On one particular day, I went by the house to drop off some things to Pauli, one of the field coordinators. It was also an elimination day. I was curious to see who would get the boot, so I stuck around to watch the results.

I was going over some paperwork with Pauli when we heard a woman yelling from above.

"Is that Tyra yelling?" I asked.

"I think so, but I've never heard her scream like that before," Pauli replied.

We ran over to the control room where we were joined by a few of our producers. Everyone was glued to the monitors as we watched Tyra scream the weave off of a contestant named Tiffany Richardson.

"Why is she so angry?" I asked Jerry, one of our crew guys.

"Tiffany just got eliminated. She didn't seem to be too broken up about it, so I guess Tyra thought she wasn't taking the competition seriously," Jerry replied.

The mood in the control room was a mix of confusion and snickers. I was siding more with the laughter. I thought it was ridiculous Tyra got so worked up over nothing, but I kept my opinions to myself.

When Season 4 came to a close, I was excited about moving into my new position until I had a meeting with my producer, Brandi. She bluntly said that working on the set of *Top Model* was a shit show and I was better off being in the office. I was about to coordinate the busiest producing team on the show. Our team handled the photo shoots and eliminations.

She also told me I would be driving around to locations all over southern California. The driving aspect had me worried about my car. My sweet little car that I had to pour a jug of water into every time I wanted to go somewhere to keep it from overheating.

I knew my car wouldn't make it through one day on *Top Model*. I wasn't in a position to buy a new car, nor did I have a down payment. But if I was going into debt, it might as well be for a dependable car. I went to a Toyota dealer and they gave me $250 for my Dodge Neon. I also pulled $300 from my savings account to add to the down payment.

My credit was less than desirable and my down payment was laughable. I could tell my gay salesman was having his doubts. I just needed to tap into an area where he would bend on businessman ethics.

He grilled me about what I did for a living and when I told him I worked on *Top Model* he squealed like a pig. He was a huge Tyra fan and that got me thinking about a possible trade.

I had an embroidered *America's Next Top Model* duffel bag that was sitting in the trunk of my car. It was a crew gift from the previous season that I never used. After a few minutes of my salesman cackling about his favorite *Top Model* episodes, I leaned over and told him about the duffel bag. I played it up by saying it was never sold publicly and only given to crew. It was brand new and I would let him have my treasured, but well crafted duffel bag if he would sell me the car I wanted.

I knew it was far from an even trade, but I hoped it would work as some kind of incentive to sway him.

After seeing the bag, he had me rolling out of there in the mini SUV I wanted in under an hour.

Thank god I traded in my old car. My production schedule on *Top Model* was relentless. I had zero days off and worked seven days a week the entire season, which lasted almost three months.

The judges on the show that season were Tyra, former model Twiggy, photographer Nigel Barker, and model/coach J. Alexander, or as we called him, "Miss J".

Twiggy and Nigel were warm and friendly. Tyra was also nice and she came with quite the entourage. Aside from her glam team and monster trailer, she also had a personal chef to cook for her on elimination days. Unfortunately, that didn't include the list of food she required from her rider. For those not familiar, a 'rider' is a list of items requested by an artist for comfort on the day of their appearance. Her rider included everything from turkey jerky, Diet Coke and raw almonds, to Red vines, Illume candles and individual trays of veggies, cheeses, and fruits.

Then there was my favorite, Miss J. He spoke his mind about everything, including his distaste for long shoot days. The studio we filmed our eliminations on had a killer cafeteria, and Miss J loved a homemade soup they had. I would bring him a bowl when I knew there would be substantial filming delays and that usually put him in better spirits.

That particular season was also the first without Janice Dickinson being a judge. I didn't meet her on the previous season because I was stuck in the office. But for season 5, they brought her back as a guest photographer on a photo shoot relating to plastic surgery, go figure.

One of the PAs went to pick her up from her home and brought her to the studios where we were having the photo shoot. My job was to meet her in front of the studios when she arrived, escort her to her dressing room and help her with anything she needed.

When the PA's car pulled up in the parking lot, I walked over to greet Janice. She opened the passenger side door and the Rolling Stones, "Sympathy For the Devil" was blaring around her as she got out of the car, singing along. I introduced myself, we shook hands and I asked her to follow me to her dressing room.

As we walked down the corridor to her dressing room, she pulled out an IPOD and some ear buds. She popped an ear bud in my ear and the other in hers, then put her arm around me and said, "You have to listen to this."

The song was "Gimme Shelter" by the Rolling Stones. Before I could say anything, she told me how she slept with Mick Jagger back in the day and what a small penis he had. She also said since she's not a judge on *Top Model* anymore, she can be the "nice one" now and doesn't have to be the bitch of the show. I smiled politely and nodded my head in agreement, hoping I was agreeing to the right thing.

I left Janice in her dressing room and walked over to a kitchen by the stage we would be shooting on. I was working on a few things when I overheard our photo director, Jay Manuel, speaking to one of the head producers of the show. He had concerns about Janice, and if she started to act up, he would leave the set. Janice and Jay hadn't seen each other yet. I took her straight to her dressing room after she arrived. I wasn't sure what issues they had in the past, but I thought it was funny how her mere presence caused such a stir.

Jay disappeared for about an hour and came back into the kitchen to speak with my producer, Brandi. He said he had a nice conversation with Janice and that everything was fine. And it was. The photo shoot went well, everyone got along and nobody walked off set.

The long hours I worked on *Top Model* overshadowed the fun of being on set. On our first elimination day, I was on set at 7:00 a.m. I didn't leave until 3:00 a.m. and had to be back by 8:00 a.m. the same morning. I literally went home, showered, fell asleep with my hair wet, slept for three hours and went right back to the set. I was half asleep when I arrived, so I used money from the show's petty cash to buy myself a large coffee. When I handed in the receipt to my Line Producer, he gave me a lecture about using show money for personal use. Lucky for him, I was too exhausted to choke him.

I calmly told him I had just come in after a near 20-hour workday. The least he could do was buy me a coffee to keep me awake, especially when they weren't paying me overtime. He relented and told me not to let it happen again. I decided that once the season wrapped, I would never come back *Top Model*. But that was only the beginning of my problems on the show.

Brandi quit halfway through the season and was replaced by a Producer named Ray. He wasn't the least bit friendly as Brandi was, and the dynamic of my producing team changed drastically when he came on board.

Aside from set experience, another reason I wanted to be a field coordinator on the show was to travel. *Top Model* always filmed the final eliminations in a different country. They went to France, Italy, Japan and recently, South Africa. I was told we were going to London. I always wanted to go to London! I didn't have a passport but paid a little extra to get it expedited before we left.

A few days before we left to London, my Line Producer told me I wouldn't be traveling abroad. He felt I wasn't cutting it as a coordinator and things would only get more hectic when they went across the pond. I was furious.

I also got into a huge fight with Ray on the day of our last photo shoot. We were filming at a house in the Valley with Steve O, Chris Pontius and Wee Man from *Jackass*. There was a delay in shuttling some of the crew from our production office to the house because of a PA who arrived late. I handled the problem and was about to tell Ray when he walked up and started yelling at me in front of the models and crew. He blamed the delay on me. I told him I handled the situation and to never scream at me like that again in front of people, and if he had an issue he should pull me aside. He was angry I talked back to him and stormed off.

Adding to that nightmare day, one of the PAs accidentally threw away the keys to our production van. Me and two other PAs had to dig through several trash bags to find them, which we did about an hour later. The only highlight of the day was meeting the guys from *Jackass*, although Steve O made me nervous. He was sweet and outgoing but quite the scatterbrain. Wee Man and Chris Pontius signed off on their appearance releases without a problem. But when I got to Steve O, I had to chase him throughout the house. He was running around with only a loincloth as I trailed him with the release and a pen. When I finally got him still, he signed across the entire page of the release. It was good enough for me. I took a quick picture with him, Wee Man and Pontius and got out of there.

We had our final elimination in Los Angeles the following day. It was a long day of filming. I didn't get home until 2:00am. I slept in the following day and made my way to our empty production offices around noon. While the crew made their way to London, I cleaned out my desk and closed out all final costs for my team. So long *Top Model*.

Shortly after leaving *Top Model*, I landed a

coordinating job on a reality show for Warner Bros. called *Survival of the Richest*. Hal Sparks, who was known for the Showtime drama *Queer as Folk*, and his numerous appearances on VH1's, *I Love the 70's, 80's and 90's* series, would be hosting the show.

I originally met Hal during my days at *Punk'd*. There were a few empty offices on our floor, so Hal and his writing partners used them while working on a pilot for VH1. I hadn't seen him since then, so I was happy when I found out he would be on the show.

A few days before we started filming, I went to visit the house where our cast would be living. Rick, one of the show's producers, made his way over to me with Hal. The moment Hal saw me he smiled, and I smiled back. Rick was about to introduce us when Hal greeted me with a big hug. He always gave the best hugs. Not one of those patronizing 'tap you on the back a few times' hugs either. But a good, hearty hug like you were family. Once he unleashed me, he told Rick, "Yeah we kind of know each other."

*Survival of the Richest* was a competition show between rich kids and poor kids with a cash prize going to the winner. Although I worked there for the entire season, the premise of the show never made sense to me. Why would rich kids care to win money when they have it? Apparently, the general public felt the same way I did. The show tanked and wasn't brought back for a second season.

When *Survival* wrapped, I landed two gigs back to back. The first was an ABC drama called *The Nine*, which starred *Boston Public* alum, Chi McBride. I didn't go up and say hi to him. Four years had passed since I worked on *Boston Public*, and I knew he wouldn't have remembered me anyway.

When I finished on *The Nine*, I started working as a staff coordinator for Graney Productions. The content of shows for Graney was different from my reality television background. They covered nature-oriented material that was geared toward networks like the Discovery Channel and Animal Planet. It wasn't a fun atmosphere like *Punk'd*, but the offices were close to home. I was also staff, which meant I didn't have to hustle every few months to find a new show to work on. Graney always had several shows filming simultaneously, so when one ended, I would hop on another.

Right when I was getting used to having a steady income, I got fired from Graney. They also fired my Production Manager, another Producer and an Editor. A few weeks after we left, I heard my Line Producer was given the axe too.

When I told some of my production folks I was looking for work, they asked about the last show I worked on. I mentioned Graney, and they gave me their sympathies. Apparently, the owners at Graney were rubbing people the wrong way in the industry. I took it as a hidden blessing that they let me go.

I was out of work for about a week or so when Eden called. Silex wanted me back. After months of working hectic production schedules, a mellow office job was exactly what I needed to refresh. I also hadn't done any work on my book since the last time I was at Silex. With the crazy hours I kept on *Top Model* and the rest of the shows, I never had time to write.

I worked at Silex for a few months. While I dodged bullets from the angry yentas that worked there, I was also able to get some solid work done on my book. I completed the outline and finished the first two chapters when I landed another show. A comedy for the FX network called *It's Always Sunny in Philadelphia*.

Unfortunately, *Sunny* had a Coordinator. The only position available was as an assistant to Tom, one of the Executive Producers. I wasn't happy about the step down in position and pay, but it was the first show I landed in months. I was also getting cabin fever at Silex, despite the progress I made on my book.

I worked on *Sunny* for two, consecutive seasons and it was a blast. Everyone was a pleasure to work with. I sat in on table readings with the cast and crew. We had catered breakfast and lunch almost every day. I couldn't believe that was my life. Another perk of my job on *Sunny* was the lighter workload. I had more down time being an assistant than I would have as a Coordinator. That gave me the opportunity to work on my book.

Tom reminded me of Dan from *Punk'd*. Both were fair but stern men with a borderline abrasive sense of humor. I developed a good working relationship with Tom, so I felt comfortable telling him I wanted to meet Danny DeVito.

I saw Danny on set, but it was always during filming. I didn't want to bother him. Tom was surprised I never met Danny before. He assumed after me being there for so long that I had.

On the morning of Danny's last day, I had mixed feelings about meeting him. I was a huge fan of his and so was my dad. We watched *Taxi* together when I was little. The show was something my dad and I bonded over, and it broke my heart he wasn't there to meet Danny.

Shortly after lunch that day, Tom took me to Danny's trailer and knocked on his door. Danny opened the door with a cracker in his hand and a few crumbs on his shirt. Tom introduced us and told him I was a big fan since the days of *Taxi*. Danny shook my hand, said it was great to meet me, and stepped out onto the ladder of his trailer.

I told him it was great to meet him too. I had a *Taxi* DVD set in my other hand that caught his eye. He smiled when he saw it and asked if he could take a look at it. He read a few of the episodes out loud and recalled various memories on set during some of those episodes.

His details of working on *Taxi* were so vivid. He spoke about them like recent memories and asked what my favorite episode was. I told him it was when Jim, played by Christopher Lloyd, got his driver's license. He laughed as he signed my DVD box and said that was a great episode. Tom took a picture of us, I thanked him for meeting me and we let him go back into his trailer.

We had the wrap party for *Sunny in Philadelphia* about a week later. I brought Britt, from Blackboard Jungle as my guest. I was in charge of planning the party, and my main stress was making sure that Danny was taken care of. I set him up with a private table and a freshly chilled bottle of premium vodka. But when he arrived, he didn't care about any of it, except for the vodka. He was down to earth and didn't want to be separated or treated like Hollywood royalty. He even chatted up Britt and I. Britt and Danny were from New Jersey, so Britt played the Jersey card. They spoke about landmarks and restaurants that were long gone.

Britt and I took a walk around the club and were standing near the dance floor when we saw Danny. He was walking in our direction and looked lost.

Britt pushed me in Danny's direction and said, "Go see what he wants!"

I walked up to Danny with a smile.

"Hi Danny, can I get you anything?" I asked.

He took a sip of his vodka on the rocks and said, "Yeah, I wanna dance. But I can't dance to this crap."

I agreed with Danny. The DJ sucked. He was blasting awful, techno music that wasn't the least bit engaging.

"What did you want to hear? I'll tell the DJ," I said.

"Something good like the Stones or James Brown," he replied.

I skipped off to the DJ booth and tapped the DJ on the shoulder.

"Hi there! I have a special request. Can you put on something like James Brown or the Rolling Stones? You're dealing with an older crowd here."

"Yeah, I can probably get to it within the hour," he replied, coldly.

"Well, Danny DeVito is here and that's what he's requesting," I said, casually.

"Wait. Danny DeVito is HERE?"

"Sure, see him over there?" I said, pointing to a nearby bar where Danny was standing.

"Holy shit. Okay, I'll play some James Brown next."

Amazing what the power of dropping a celebrity name will get you. The DJ cut off the current song that was playing and mixed it into "Make it Funky" by James Brown. Within moments, Danny walked onto the dance floor and started shaking his ass by himself.

I asked Britt if he wanted to dance. He told me not to let Danny dance by himself and pushed me toward the dance floor. I shrugged my shoulders and walked over to dance with Danny. Shortly after "Make it Funky" ended, the DJ played "Jumping Jack Flash" by the Rolling Stones. Boy could Danny cut up a rug. He loved his classic rock and so did the rest of the crew. It was the first time the floor had been packed since the party started.

I could have come back for future seasons of *Sunny*, but my finances were suffering from the drop in pay. The show's Coordinator wasn't going anywhere either, so I reluctantly gave up my job with Tom. I visit the set from time to time, but I haven't worked on the show again, unfortunately.

I went back to Silex for a few weeks after wrapping on Sunny. I did more work done on my book, and it wasn't long before I landed a coordinating job on an MTV show called *Nitro Circus*. It was a stunt show featuring a cast of bike riders, stunt performers and base jumpers led by Motorsports competitor, Travis Pastrana. Dickhouse Productions produced the show. They were also responsible for hits like *Jackass, Fantasy Factory,* and *Rob and Big*. Working on *Nitro Circus* was fun, but mildly stressful for several reasons.

One being, that we worked in the same building as the Dickhouse guys. Most of the crew working on *Nitro Circus* had previously worked on *Jackass*, so the practice of pulling pranks was commonplace in our office. I usually saw the guys booby-trapping something in the office at least once a week. On one occasion, it was a boxing glove the size of a beach ball that was set to come down in one of the doorways. Another time, the guys unscrewed all the bolts on one of our producer's office chairs. Guys were the main targets and generally not the girls, but I was still paranoid.

The other source of my stress was the stunts our cast performed. There wasn't a guarantee they would succeed and several times they didn't.

On one occasion Erik Roner, our base jump expert, was supposed to jump off a Russian swing and land into a pile of foam and cups. But when he jumped, he accidentally slid off and landed in the path of where the swing was coming down. He quickly scurried to get out of the way, but the swing still grazed him on one of his sides. He complained his ribs hurt after the stunt, so I immediately took him to the hospital.

Another time, Greg "Special Greg" Powell, Travis' cousin, injured his shoulder and wrist from another stunt. I had to take him to the hospital too. I can't count how many times I cancelled my personal plans to accompany cast members to the emergency room. I visited Cedars Sinai Hospital more times during that show than I had in my entire life.

But the event that freaked me out while working on *Nitro Circus* didn't involve a stunt. It occurred with a cast member during an out-of-town shoot in Utah.

A few of us went back to the hotel's Jacuzzi after a long day of filming. I was gathering my things and saying goodbye to the guys when a cast member, who I'll call "Sam", approached me. He said he was leaving too and would escort me to my room.

Sam had been flirting with me on that trip, but it was usually after a few cocktails. He walked me to my room and told me about a trick one of the crew guys taught him. He started to unscrew the peephole in my door without asking me. His story sounded odd. I was also exhausted and didn't care what he was talking about. He unscrewed the peephole about halfway when I told him to show me another time. I wanted to shower and go to bed. We said our goodbyes and he walked away, or so I thought.

I took a hot shower and left the bathroom door open to let out the steam. When I was drying myself off, I heard noises at my door. I wrapped myself in a towel and peeked out from the bathroom. The noises sounded similar to when Sam was messing with the peephole in my door. I stared at it for a few moments, and it looked different to me. Somehow, Sam managed to unscrew the peephole while I was showering and flip it around. This gave him a wide-angle view of everything in my hotel room. I was mortified.

A few moments later, there was a gentle knock on my hotel door. I froze.

I slowly closed my bathroom door and quickly got dressed. Once fully clothed, I crawled out of the bathroom and put my finger over the peephole. If Sam's eye was looking back at me, I was fully prepared to open the door and promptly punch him in his perverted face.

He gently knocked a few more times. I looked through the peephole but he had his finger over it. I quietly tiptoed back to my bathroom until I heard him walk away a few minutes later. Once I felt the coast was clear, I opened my hotel door. He was nowhere to be found. I quickly reversed the peephole to its original position and jumped into bed.

Shortly after midnight, Sam sent me a text saying, *"I'm lonely, can I stay in your room tonight?"*

Clearly, he wasn't coming to my room to play a round of Parcheesi. I couldn't believe he had the nerve to send me something so bold. I ignored his text and tried to work on my book.

He texted me again about ten minutes later and apologized. I didn't respond to that either. He texted me a third time, almost a half hour later saying, *"I'm a stupid ass wasn't acting right, sorry."*

I never responded to Sam's texts. I just sat in bed, thinking about how to handle the situation when I saw him on set the next day.

After a choppy night of sleep, I met my crew in the hotel lobby the following morning. We were filming a human slingshot stunt at a personal residence about an hour away.

When we arrived at the location, there was a large, log cabin style home that sat on about an acre of land. A large veranda wrapped around the exterior of the house, and the fields were plush and green as far as the eye could see. The property was beautiful. It took the edge off of any stress I was feeling from the night before.

I sat on a porch swing on the back veranda and

pulled out my laptop to do some work. It was a sunny day, so I put my sunglasses on. I took a glance around the property and noticed Sam lingering by the craft service table. He spotted me and started to make his way toward me. I pretended I didn't see him and put my focus back to my laptop.

Sam took a seat next to me and apologized for sending the texts. He never mentioned anything about reversing the peephole though. I wasn't sure if he intentionally left that part out or maybe he was so drunk he didn't remember doing it. Had we been in a personal setting, I would have ripped him a new one without question. But this was work. I needed to be professional. We had one day left of filming before the show wrapped for the season. He seemed remorseful, so I let it go. If I felt he was a threat to any of the girls who worked on the show, I would have told someone. But I never did.

Sam didn't speak to me for the rest of the day. He also kept his distance the following day when we came back to Los Angeles. I saw him briefly at our wrap party about a week later, but other than a wave hello, he never spoke to me again.

MTV didn't renew *Nitro Circus* for a third season. But it did go on to have success as a live action sports show. Travis and most of the original cast still perform at various arenas and stadiums around the world.

After wrapping up on *Nitro Circus*, I took a solid week off to lie in bed and recover from the hectic filming schedule. It wasn't long before I landed a Travel Coordinator job on an ABC show called *Dancing With the Stars*.

*Dancing With the Stars* was the largest show I ever coordinated. I was used to knowing the names of every crewmember from the small productions I worked on, but this show was a monster. Coordinating all the travel became my worst nightmare.

I never had a moment of downtime on that show. I was constantly working overtime, and the biggest travel pains in my ass were celebrity cast members Evan Lysacek and Kate Gosselin.

Evan himself wasn't difficult; he was sweet and humble. The issue was his schedule. Aside from *Dancing With the Stars*, he was also performing with a touring show called *Stars on Ice*. When he finished a *Stars on Ice* performance, I would fly him to Los Angeles to rehearse and perform on *Dancing with the Stars*. The moment he finished on *Dancing With the Stars*, I would fly him out to whatever city the *Stars on Ice* tour was performing next. This happened on a weekly basis over the period of a few months.

The problem with Kate Gosselin was Kate Gosselin. She was high maintenance and wanted limos to pick her up from the airport when she flew home to the East Coast, or came to L.A. for the show. Her travel plans made me postal, especially when she made last minute decisions to bring her litter of kids into town.

Working on *Dancing With the Stars* was bittersweet. I was grateful for the experience and it was nice getting my friends tickets to the shows. But I felt I was given the short end of the stick and so did several other crew members I befriended. It didn't help that they gave me two days to wrap up the show, when it would have taken any normal person almost a week.

I asked my supervisor for one additional wrap day. They denied my request. I worked the extra day anyway, completely unpaid because I wanted to be professional and leave my paperwork in order.

I knew I would never go back to *Dancing With the Stars*, although a few of the producers said they would bring me back the following season.

Funny enough, when the next season started prepping, they never sent me an email to come back. C'est la vie.

# 6

# MY BIOLOGICAL CLOCK
# IS SET TO SNOOZE

*F*or anyone who has wanted to work in the wacky world of television, let me offer you this information, which may change your mind about seeking employment in this industry.

For starters, this is not a 9 to 5 occupation. It's more of a 'come in early and you'll leave whenever your work is done for the day' kind of job. If you're not ready to bust your ass and take initiative, don't bother trying to work in this industry. And most importantly, the cardinal rule you NEVER want to ask on any set is, "When can I leave?" That is a loaded question that may cause your Producer to unleash a downpour of fire and brimstone upon you.

The other downside is job stability. You need to hustle and make a good name for yourself in this industry, because as big as it is, it's also a small world. Everyone knows everyone in some capacity. Most people get production jobs through recommendations, and if word spreads that you're lazy or a complainer, you can bet your time in the entertainment industry will be cut short.

Another thing to remember is that life on set is not glamorous. If you think you're going to stroll into a location and hang out with actors for the afternoon, think again. The reality is you'll probably have five production assistants running around town trying to find some rare gluten free bullshit meal in order to keep your actor or other talent from flipping out.

And in all that chaos, you'll be lucky to have a social life, as was the case for yours truly. But I wasn't looking to procreate during that time, mainly because the men in my life were far from father material.

First there was Ramone. He was the drummer of a band called Jumper. We met through Pandora while he was in town visiting from San Francisco. We started dating shortly before I booked *Top Model*, and boy, was he a looker. He shared a striking resemblance to Brandon Boyd from Incubus. Along with his good looks came a cheeky sense of humor. I was immediately smitten.

I probably shouldn't use the term "dating" with Ramone. It wasn't a relationship either. I don't know what the hell it was. I suppose some made up terminology from the *Twilight Zone* could be used to describe it. But it continues to be one of the oddest encounters I've had with any man to this day.

Sure, Ramone was good looking. He was also funny and seemed nice enough. But once I got to know him, I realized what a little bitch he was. It was like hanging out with a neurotic girlfriend. He would get ideas in his head about things and act out in a passive aggressive way. He also got butt hurt over the simplest things. I found that strange because he was the master at dishing out jokes and making fun of people. Don't get me wrong; he could take a good joke. But if you struck a nerve with him, he would completely shut down and cut you off for an undetermined period of time.

If I confronted Ramone about something he didn't want to deal with, he would disappear. He wouldn't return my calls, texts, or emails until he got over whatever he was upset about. Then he would call out of the blue and act like everything was fine. I never met a straight guy who acted like a bitchy girl before. If anyone went through a freeze out at the hands of Ramone, Pandora and I called it "riding the Ramonercoaster."

Ramone and I hung out a few times over several months, but we never made out once. The one time I kissed him, he stiffened his lips like I was forcing him to take medicine he didn't want. I never tried to kiss him again and he didn't try either. He also didn't like any form of affection, whether it be public or private.

Another issue was his obsession with porn. If he were a teenage boy, it might have been understandable. But he was 35. He constantly watched porn and was obsessed with hand jobs for some reason. He even went to out-of-state porn conventions and befriended a few female adult stars.

Ramone and I hung out off and on for about three months. We had sex once, and that was the straw that broke the camel's back, no pun intended.

On our first and only night together, he had porn playing in the background and wanted me to mimic the positions in the movie. I like to consider myself an open-minded person. If he were my boyfriend, I would have been up for some role-playing. But I sensed something off about Ramone that went beyond his aversion to physical affection. And as a result of him not being comfortable, it made me uncomfortable. It didn't help that he was ordering me around like a drill sergeant either. Sex is supposed to be fun and spontaneous, or slow and sensual. I felt like I was spending a night away at boot camp.

Nothing about our sexual encounter was pleasurable. When it was done, he put a body pillow between us and passed out. I would have left that night had I not been exhausted. After a choppy night of sleep, I skipped out of there the following morning.

Next on the list of dating disasters was a brief rendezvous with a young buck named Pete. We met through Pixie while I was working on *Sunny in Philadelphia*. I don't know what I was thinking on that one. He was barely in his 20s and acted his age. He looked like a lanky skater kid with his long, platinum blond bangs. We went out a handful of times, had a few romps, and then he began to distance himself. He didn't contact me for a week, and I knew the party was over. I wasn't angry or upset about it. I knew it wouldn't last long anyway.

Pete emailed me two weeks later and apologized for being incommunicado. He said he was in Vegas, marrying his newly pregnant ex-girlfriend.

I read his email at work, shortly before I went into a table reading for *Sunny*. I wasn't heartbroken by what Pete said, but I was grossed out that he was hooking up with his ex while dating me. Strangely though, the amount of laughing I did during my table reading put me in a better mood. It took the edge off of any negative feelings I had toward Pete. I was able to see things clearly. Not that I agreed with what he did. It was a dick move, pun intended. But he admitted he was wrong.

I eventually forgave Pete for being a pig. He was young anyway and we all make mistakes. After being with him, I swore off dating anyone under the age of

30. I also told myself I would never date within my circle of friends again.

Then there was Nick, the pint-sized folk singer. He stood about 5'5". I think I outweighed him by a few pounds. He was soft spoken but sweet. We met at a dive bar in Hollywood where his band was performing on a warm, summer evening.

Nick's music was a bit out of my realm. I dated musicians before, but they were always rockers. The first time I saw Nick perform, he had a harmonica neck rack around his head and only played acoustic guitar.

Nick lived in a small bungalow on a chunk of property in Angeles National Forest. His drummer, Robb, purchased the land with inheritance left by his recently deceased mother. There were two additional bungalows on the property, which his other band mates resided in. Robb lived in the main house that looked like a log cabin.

I dated Nick for about two months and only went to his place once. He always told me how much he enjoyed living up in the forest with his band mates. When he finally invited me to see his bungalow, I looked forward to a well-needed evening out of the city.

Nick mentioned it was tricky finding the property. He gave me the address of a market at the bottom of the mountain and told me to meet him there. I assumed his invitation meant it was going to be the two of us. But when I saw his jeep pull into the driveway of the market with his band manager, Holland, I was mildly annoyed.

Holland and I met a few times at Nick's shows. She followed him around like a puppy dog and was always by his side, especially when I was around. Nick referred to her as the band manager, even though she had no experience in management. She was an out-of-work actress that befriended the band and was somehow designated to be their manager. To me, she was a glorified den mother. I wasn't happy she came along with Nick on what I thought was going to be a date.

Robb's property could only be accessed by a single road along Angeles Crest Highway, which took you through a stunning twenty-minute scenic route of the mountainside. After some tricky turns from the main road, we reached the property. I watched Nick's jeep disappear up a narrow, dirt driveway with a steep incline. My mini SUV barely made it up without tipping over.

Holland walked into one of the bungalows, while Nick gave me a tour of the property. All three bungalows were nestled near each other at the top of the driveway. The main house was set at the bottom and could be accessed by a small walkway behind the bungalows, or sliding your ass down the driveway. Nick pointed to each bungalow and told me where each band member lived. Naturally, the bungalow Holland disappeared into was his.

We walked into Nick's and his band mates were there, along with a few of their friends. Some were sitting on a small futon, others were scattered about the floor or sitting on whatever piece of furniture they could in the small, studio-sized bungalow.

One of his band members pulled out some bongos and Holland grabbed a tambourine. Nick picked up his acoustic guitar and began to sing.

They were a nice group of people, but it was too 'kumbaya' for me. I grew up on the Sunset Strip for Christ sake. I was loud and cracked inappropriate jokes. I liked to do shots of vodka and throw my devil horns in the air. Nick was one of the sweetest guys I dated in a long time, but being around his crowd was a snore fest. I felt like I couldn't be myself. Everyone was always calm and in a Zen state of mind. Nick and I called it quits shortly after my visit.

A few weeks after my breakup with Nick, I went to San Diego with Roxy, a girl I knew through Pixie. Roxy loved the band Incubus as much as I did. When we heard they had a show in San Diego, we planned a road trip.

Vosbury, the opening band, was playing when we arrived. I wasn't familiar with their music. I only knew they had a hit on the radio and were from the east coast.

Roxy and I were wired after the Incubus show. The last thing we wanted to do was go back to our hotel room and stare at each other. She suggested we sneak backstage. I told her she was nuts, and followed her around the venue to where the tour buses were parked.

There were two guards standing by a flimsy arm gate. We sat down on a nearby curb and talked for about a half hour when we saw the guards walk away. We assumed they would be back soon, so we ducked under the gate and briskly made our way toward the tour buses.

The first person that passed us was Jose Pasillas, the drummer of Incubus. Roxy took a picture with him but wanted to know where the singer, Brandon Boyd, was. After taking a stroll around the buses with no sight of him, we assumed he was already on the tour bus.

While we mumbled back and forth on what to do, a rockabilly-looking guy approached us. He introduced himself as Logan, the drummer of Vosbury. He looked like Gavin Rossdale from Bush, except with a black pompadour similar to Elvis Presley.

Logan was from New York and stood about 5' 10" with hazel eyes. He was slightly awkward and looked a bit tipsy. After chatting for a few minutes, he invited us onto Vosbury's tour bus for a cocktail.

Roxy and I were having drinks with Logan and some of his band mates when his bus driver came in. The bus would be leaving momentarily.

"Where are you guys off to now?" I asked Logan.

"We're going to Vegas. You guys should come!" Logan replied, enthusiastically.

"That sounds like fun, but I don't have the time or gas to get there."

"So, just ride with us on the bus."

"You're crazy. My car is here, how would we get home from Vegas?"

"Come on, it would be fun! We're going for the *MTV Video Music Awards*!"

Roxy chimed in and wanted to go to Vegas. Being that I was five years older than her, I knew this was nothing more than drunken talk on behalf of Logan.

Sure it sounded exciting, but everything is fun when you're drunk. Reality would set in the next day when we sobered up, and Logan would look at us like two stray animals he wouldn't know what to do with.

I didn't want to ruin a fun adventure, but I knew I had to be the voice of reason. More importantly, neither of us had money to get ourselves back to L.A. If we did, I would have taken Logan up on his offer. Instead, I thanked him for the invitation and said we would have to pass. The tour bus started up with us on it and swung by the parking lot to drop us off at my car.

Although I didn't make it to Vegas, Logan and I exchanged numbers before he left. He was coming to L.A. and wanted to see me while he was in town.

A few weeks later, Vosbury headlined a sold out show at the Wiltern Theatre in Los Angeles. Logan left me passes at the box office, and I took Roxy with me.

When we arrived at the Wiltern, I had passes and tickets waiting for me as promised by Logan. But when we tried to go backstage, we were stopped by security. Apparently, our passes were not all access. They were only for an after party in one of the green rooms, and we couldn't go backstage until after the show.

I was annoyed at first, but it made sense. I had just met Logan. I shouldn't have been so entitled to think I deserved an all-access pass to his show. That would probably come with time.

Yes, I'll admit it was exciting to watch Logan on stage while the crowd jumped around. I had dated many musicians, but none of them made a living playing music like Logan. They were usually in garbage bands that did the Hollywood club rotation and never went anywhere.

Roxy and I went to the party backstage after the show. We were chatting with some of the guys in Vosbury when Logan walked up and gave me a hug. He thanked me for coming to the show and asked how I liked their set. I was about to answer when a skinny blonde with short hair interrupted our conversation. She looked to be in her late 20s and leapt on Logan with the enthusiasm of a hyper puppy.

"I have someone I need you to meet, you HAVE to come with me right now!" she squealed.

Annoyed by her rudeness, I stared at her.

"Hi, I'm Danica," she said, smiling at me. "I'll bring him right back. Promise!" she continued, as she grabbed Logan by the arm and dragged him off.

I wasn't going to wait around like a dog. I told Roxy if he wasn't back by the time we finished our drinks, we were leaving.

Ten minutes later, Logan was nowhere to be found. I texted him to say I was leaving. He replied shortly after I dropped off Roxy and apologized for his abrupt departure. He also mentioned he was coming back in L.A. in a few weeks. Vosbury was voted 'Artist of the Week' on MTV, so they were filming a few TV spots for the network. I accepted his apology and agreed to meet him when he came back to town.

Meanwhile, the identity of Danica was digging at me. She seemed to be fairly comfortable running up to Logan and interrupting us the way she did. I did what any other woman would do in the age of the Internet. I did a Google search with Logan's name and hers to see what showed up, and it wasn't long before I had my answer.

The first thing that came up was a picture of them on the red carpet at the *MTV Video Music Awards.* I also found out that Danica's father was the guitarist of a well-known band from the '70s. She was an aspiring singer and guitar player too, but her only claim to fame was her famous father.

Vosbury came to town a few weeks later. I met Logan in the lobby of his hotel on Highland Avenue, and we walked across the street to Shintaro, his favorite sushi restaurant. Not being one to beat around the bush, I asked him about Danica. He said they dated in the past, but there was nothing going on between them currently. He ran into her on MTV's red carpet with her father, which explained the pictures. I found his reasoning understandable but it stayed in the back of my mind.

And speaking of exes, it wasn't long before one of my own reared his jealous, little head.

Ramone and I hadn't spoken much since our disastrous sexual encounter. That quickly changed when he found out about Logan. He started texting me dirty jokes to engage me in conversation. I felt they were stupid and inappropriate. I told him that on several occasions and it only egged him on. When I stopped responding, he told me I was stuck up because I was dating a 'rock star'.

Ramone's whiplash personality changes were common. If he were bitchy, I let it go to avoid "riding the Ramonercoaster". But when he started taking digs at Logan, I had enough. I didn't care if he got upset. The only way to shut him up was to hit him where it hurt, and that was right in his drumsticks.

Logan and Ramone were drummers. I knew it bothered Ramone that Logan was a successful, touring drummer. The next time he started ragging on Logan, I told him he was jealous because Logan was a better drummer than he was. On another occasion, I said Logan could give him drumming lessons for a small fee. That sent Ramone right over the edge, and I happily boarded the "Ramonercoaster".

I was enjoying a few months of peace and quiet when I saw Ramone at a show in Malibu. Pandora was with me, and I was still dating Logan. He didn't immediately come up to me. I talked with a few friends while Pandora walked over to chat with him. I knew she would get the dirt. Sure enough, she did and told me about it over a glass of wine.

"He's a little apprehensive about coming over," she said.

"Well, he should be. He's been acting like a jealous bitch for the last few months over Logan," I replied, bluntly.

"He said it was just jokes and that you took it the wrong way."

"Oh bullshit. It's straight up passive aggressive behavior."

"Are you going to talk to him?"

"Only if he comes over. He brought this all on himself. If I go over like everything is cool, that is pacifying his ridiculous behavior."

Ramone eventually came up to me that night. It was the first time I saw him be somewhat remorseful, although he didn't apologize for his behavior. We briefly spoke about Logan and he insisted that I took his jokes the wrong way. I knew he would never admit to being jealous, and I didn't care enough to argue about it anyway. I told him that moving forward, the subject of Logan was off limits. He reluctantly agreed.

I dated Logan off and on for about three years, but we weren't exclusive. It was something we never discussed. I knew shortly after we started dating, that I didn't want him as a boyfriend for a variety of reasons.

For one, he was unintentionally flaky. I think he had a mild case of A.D.D. He was a sweet guy but going to his shows was mildly stressful for me. It was always a crapshoot on whether I would be on his guest list. I know it sounds like I'm being a diva, but how hard is it to remember to put a person on a list? I usually had all-access passes waiting for me when I arrived. But on a few occasions, I didn't have any passes or my name was misspelled and I had to convince the venue that I was the botched person on the list.

Why did I put up with it? Well, I had nothing better to do and Logan was fun to hang out with. He was laid back and never got angry over anything, which was the polar opposite of Ramone's neurosis. It was an easy situation that didn't require any serious emotional attachment. It was also nice dating someone who had a steady income and paid for everything.

Going to Logan's shows (when there wasn't a list issue) was an added bonus. Vosbury were reaching their peak when Logan and I began dating. I had all-access passes to the biggest shows and festivals all over Southern California.

Needless to say, after a few years of dating, things became stale between Logan and me. I knew that was inevitable. We cared for each other, but we were never in love. His pseudo A.D.D was also getting to me. I constantly had to repeat things I already told him. But the worst issue was his on again/off again problem with alcohol.

It was rare when Logan had a few drinks and let the effects taper off. When he drank, he would usually binge drink. Most people would pass out after an abundance of alcohol. But for Logan, it gave him energy like drinking a case of Red Bull. He was never an angry or obnoxious drunk though. He kept his same cheery demeanor, only sloppier.

He went through periods where he stopped drinking completely. He worked out everyday when he was off tour and said how great it felt to have alcohol out of his system. He freely admitted he was an alcoholic, and did go to few A.A. meetings on occasion. That only lasted until a band related event or show took place. He wouldn't dive in with a drink or two either; it was right back to binge mode.

During the last few months we dated, our calls and texts dwindled down considerably. Adding that to his ongoing drinking problem, I knew our time together had to end. Logan mentioned that Vosbury was coming to L.A. to play the upcoming *Projekt Revolution* festival. I planned on telling him then.

I arrived at the Verizon Wireless Amphitheater in Irvine and walked to the will call booth. One thing I wouldn't miss was the roulette game of whether I would be on Vosbury's guest list or not. Go figure, I was and with an all-access pass too.

I glanced at the set times and realized Vosbury was about to go on. I jogged through the backstage area and up a ramp with a side view that overlooked the stage.

When Vosbury finished their set, I walked over to their tour bus. Logan gave me with a hearty hug and escorted me to a lounge at the back of the bus. It was the perfect time to have "the talk" with Logan. We sat down and shared a moment of uncomfortable silence. That's when I knew he was going to end things with me too.

"Okay this is weird, so I'm just going to talk turkey with you okay?" I said, bluntly.

"Sounds good to me," Logan replied with a slight laugh.

"We haven't talked much over the last few months and you've been distant. I'm guessing this is over or you're seeing someone else. Am I right?"

"Um yeah...I've kinda started seeing someone recently..."

He paused and looked at me like a little kid who had just broken a dish.

"I'm sorry. Is it bad to tell you that?" he asked, shyly.

I laughed and said, "Of course not. You're being honest. I want you to be happy. I want us both to be happy."

"You're not acting how I thought you would."

"Did you want me to cry, scream and throw drumsticks at you?"

"I guess that's what I'm used to."

"With this girl or past girlfriends?"

"Both," he said sounding defeated.

Any small part of me that was upset over him dating this girl was thrown out the window in the name of good gossip.

"Okay, spill it. Give me all the *chisme*," I said.

"What's *chisme*?" he asked.

"It's Spanish for 'gossip.'"

"Well...she lives nearby, but she comes over everyday," he said, flustered.

"So you're dating but you don't want to see her everyday? I don't understand."

"Me either. I don't want a girlfriend right now, but she's over every day, even when I don't ask her to come over."

"That sounds intense."

"It is. So I don't think it's right if I see you

180

anymore because I'm really attracted to you and she's very possessive."

"How possessive?" I asked.

"Well, she threatened to cut me if I ever cheated on her, so I'm a little scared of her," he said with a nervous laugh.

"And you see nothing wrong with that?" I asked, raising both of my eyebrows.

"I guess it's a little much. Look, I've always had a good time with you and like I said before, I'm really attracted to you. But it would be wrong to see you when I'm in the middle of this. I don't want to be the cheating boyfriend. If I'm with you, I won't have a good time because I'll be dodging her calls. It's a jerky thing to do to you and her," he said.

Although I had a hard time believing Logan could be bullied into a relationship, I had to give him credit for being honest. He could have easily pulled double duty, considering her and I lived on opposite coasts.

"I think you're as crazy as she is to stay in that relationship, but it's your life," I said, sarcastically.

"Thanks for being really cool about all this," he replied.

We walked off the bus while Chris Cornell howled through his set. It was getting cold out so Logan gave me his official *Projekt Revolution* hoodie. He said to remind him to get it back before I left.

After getting something to eat, we went back to the main stage to see Linkin Park play. I felt sad standing next to Logan as we watched their set. Sure, there was no future for us romantically, but I still cared for him. We had many great times together and it was fun watching Vosbury grow as a band over the last few years.

When Linkin Park finished, Logan walked me to my car. He apologized for any weirdness. I told him it was fine and wished him the best with his new girlfriend. I forgot to give him his *Project Revolution* hoodie back that night, but it sits in my closet to this day should he ever ask for it.

I'm glad that things ended when they did with Logan. That experience taught me a valuable lesson and so did dating Nick, Pete and even Ramone. I was never going to find a good man if I kept wasting my time with "filler" guys. I knew they weren't boyfriend material but I dated them because I felt it was better than being alone.

I spent years giving dating advice to my girlfriends on how they deserved men better than the ones they were dating. I should have followed my own advice. I was a hypocrite and a walking contradiction. It was perfectly fine to be alone, and shortly after I came to that realization, everything started to fall into place.

I landed an awesome full time job by my place as a staff coordinator for Fireline, a video game marketing company. Sure, I would miss the world of television, but I was trading that in for job stability, health insurance and paid vacation days. It wasn't a nine to five office job either. There would be no timecards or set lunch times. My workload dictated my hours. I could dress however I wanted and take lunch whenever I was hungry. The president of the company was also a Howard Stern fan. He had no problem with me listening to the show at my desk every morning. It didn't get any better. Actually, it did.

During my first week at Fireline, my supervisor, Sally, asked if I had a passport. She wanted to send me to London for a shoot the following week! I couldn't believe it. London as in England, as in the country where my favorite band, The Beatles hailed from!

I also spoke with my friend Gavin, who was the drummer in a band called Jaybird. They were currently touring Europe and had a show in London on the day I was set to leave. After doing a price comparison, staying an extra day wasn't going to cost me anything extra. I changed my ticket and planned to fly out the morning after the Jaybird show.

The trip couldn't have come at a better time. I had rid myself of all the useless men in my life. Putting an ocean between them and myself was exactly what I needed to wipe the slate clean.

I was so antsy that I stayed awake for the entire flight to London. And because of the eight-hour time difference, I watched an entire day pass before my eyes. It was like being in a time machine. The sun was high in the sky when I boarded the plane. When we crossed the Atlantic Ocean, I watched it race across the sky into a beautiful sunset and spring back as a lovely sunrise.

After landing at Heathrow Airport, we checked into an airport hotel nearby. It was about 8:00 a.m. U.K. time. We had a meeting with our London crew later that afternoon. The plan was to get some rest until they could take us to our hotel in Warwickshire, about two hours north of London.

After checking into our hotel, I was the first to say I was hungry. The concierge kindly directed us to the dining area of the hotel.

The dining room had a breakfast bar and a chef with a small grill off to the side. The breakfast bar had fruit, along with some strange items like half roasted tomatoes, whole sautéed mushrooms, and their version of bacon, which looked like slices of ham. It looked more like a dinner bar than anything else.

I walked up to the chef and requested an omelet. I felt it was a safe bet. It takes effort to mess up scrambled eggs.

I went back to the breakfast bar to get some fruit while my omelet was made. When I walked back to the chef, he handed me a feast fit for a hamster.

Keep in mind, I'm not a person who can eat big portions of food, but what I received was a one-egg omelet. The first I've ever eaten in my life. My producer and director laughed when they saw it. I finished it in two bites. Rather than be a glutton and ask for a second omelet, I went to my room and took a well-needed nap.

I woke up a few hours later and it wasn't long before our London crew arrived. After driving us to our hotel in Warwickshire, we ate a hefty Thai dinner before crashing out for our shoot early the next morning.

After stuffing ourselves with a hearty breakfast, our crew drove us out to Rare. Rare was a video game development company nestled on a plush, green countryside. It was breathtaking. I couldn't imagine going to a place like that everyday. Talk about a stress-free work environment!

Our shoot ran smooth as butter that day. We filmed three sit down interviews, which we finished in a few hours. With our work done in Warwickshire, we had no reason to stay there another night, so we went to our hotel in London. I was happy to find we were staying at St. Martins Lane, a luxury five star hotel located in the West End. My room had floor-to-ceiling windows and a spectacular view of the city.

Shortly after getting acclimated, I met my producer and director in the lobby so we could find a place to have dinner.

As we strolled around the streets looking for a restaurant, we walked through Trafalgar Square. We also passed by the infamous London Eye, and Big Ben, the mighty clock tower. Both had a stunning interchanging light show.

We walked around for about an hour when we

came across a less populated area. The roads were narrow and I drank in the historic architecture of the buildings surrounding me. I felt like I was on the set of a Jack the Ripper movie. I could feel the age of the city as I stumbled through its old, cobblestone streets.

Shortly after we sat down for dinner, I received an email that our shoot for the following day was cancelled. I was stoked! I had two days to explore the city!

I knew one person in London. A girl named Raine, who I befriended years earlier during her brief visit to Los Angeles. Raine was a punked out version of Rainbow Brite. She was a petite little thing that wore colorful clothes to match her multicolored dreadlocks. I told her I was coming to town, and she was more than happy to show me the sights of the city.

Raine met me at my hotel the following day and dragged me all over London. We took pictures by Big Ben, James Park, Buckingham Palace, Carnaby Street, and Piccadilly Circus. After an early dinner, we finished the night off at a rocker bar called The Intrepid Fox. It reminded me of a British version of the Rainbow on the Sunset Strip.

I ordered pear ciders for Raine and I while she grabbed a table. I tipped the bartender two British pounds and he looked at me like I gave him a piece of gold. I told Raine about his strange look and she told me that they don't tip in the U.K. The bar was packed when I grabbed our second round of drinks, but my smiling bartender picked me out of the crowd and asked what I wanted. I grabbed two more pair ciders and tipped him again. I eventually ordered two more rounds from him, and every time I came near the bar, I got my drinks immediately, regardless of who was ahead of me.

After four rounds of pear ciders between us,

Raine and I were ready to call it a night. Her apartment, or as she called it, a 'flat', was a ten minute walk from the bar. I had no idea where I was or my hotel for that matter. She sweetly informed me it was a twenty-minute cab ride away and she flagged down a cab for me. She also said to get a good nights rest because she was taking me to Abbey Road the following day!

I returned to my room around 11:00 p.m. It was my last night on that side of London and having my hotel be paid for by Fireline. I would be moving to a modest hotel in Camden Locke the following day, about fifteen minutes away. It was also my last chance to capture the evening lights of the London Eye and Big Ben because the Jaybird show was the following evening.

The wind was brisk as I walked through Trafalgar Square. I snapped a few pictures of its glorious statues and continued to the London Eye that sits on the South Bank of the River Thames. I strolled over to Big Ben and noticed the streets were looking sparse as I grabbed a few pictures. I heard the West End was safe, but I wasn't going to take my chances. I briskly made my way back to the hotel and took a well-needed shower.

My growling stomach woke me up early the next morning. Rather than order room service, I got off my ass and explored the area around my hotel. I loved the cobblestone streets. I thought the streets of New York felt old, but it was nothing in comparison to the West End.

The scent of eggs and ham lured my nose two blocks away to a little café. After grabbing a breakfast sandwich, I went back to the hotel to enjoy the last few hours in my comfy five-star room.

As I picked through my breakfast, I turned on the BBC news channel. In all of my excitement about coming to London over the last few days, I forgot I would be there on September 11th.

I felt a little sad not being in The States on one of the darkest days in my country's history. I flipped through several news stations. I was curious to get an outside, non-American perspective on the events surrounding 9/11.

What I saw was a repeating news story on some dumb Florida preacher whose name I won't mention. He was a religious zealot who planned on having a rally that day to burn the Quran. Everyone was up in arms about it, not just the Muslims. That's when I got a little worried. I was an American in a foreign country, and here's this other American making us look bad by being a loudmouth. Being outside the U.S. was not where I wanted to be at that moment. Not that I felt I was in any serious danger, but it was something that stuck in the back of my head.

About an hour later, it was time to check out of St. Martins Lane. I gathered my things and took a cab to my new hotel near the Camden Locke Marketplace.

Raine arrived shortly after I did and took me on a brief stroll through the open-air marketplace. It was filled with stalls, shops, pubs and restaurants that reminded me of shopping on Melrose in Hollywood. After a few minutes of window-shopping, she guided us to the nearest Tube station, London's equivalent to a subway system. We were going to Abbey Road!

When we arrived at the small intersection of where Abbey Road Studios stood, there were twenty people or so sprinkled around the area. Some were getting their picture taken on the infamous walkway while blocking traffic. Locals showed their distaste for the disruption by incessantly honking their horns.

The walkway was busy, so I killed time by leaving my mark on the graffiti covered wall in front of Abbey Road Studios. I pulled out a black marker and drew a peace sign on the wall as Raine took pictures of me. I wrote my name and "USA" inside the peace sign along with the current date of "9/11/10".

After signing the wall, we took a stroll around the walkway to see what the best angle would be for my picture. The angle similar to the Abbey Road album would require Raine to stand in the middle of the street. There was a lot of traffic that day and I didn't want her to be road kill. After looking around a little more I noticed a tiny island off to the side. It would provide a great angle for a picture, so I had Raine stand there while I ran across the street.

I wasn't halfway across Abbey Road when some asshole started walking up behind me. He looked to be in his late 40s and was bitching at a guy he was with to take his picture on the walkway.

"Will you get the hell off the street! I'm trying to get my picture taken!" I yelled.

"I'm trying to get my picture too!" the guy yelled back.

I could tell by his accent he was American.

"So? Give me a minute to take mine and then you can get yours! I was here first anyway. Damn rude ass American!" I yelled.

A group of people standing on the curb around him started laughing. I could also hear Raine howling from across the street.

The guy reluctantly backed off and stood at the curb with his arms crossed. I took another walk across while Raine snapped a few pictures. She quickly glanced at them and gave me the thumbs up. Unfortunately, the best quality photo was the one with that loudmouth in it. But he was far enough away for me to crop him out of the picture.

We grabbed lunch by my hotel and I mentioned I was going to the Water Rats Theatre for a show that night. It turns out that Raine was a huge Jaybird fan, so we planned on meeting there later.

When I came back to the hotel, I had a few hours to kill and thought about the evening ahead of me. After a night out with Raine and Gavin, I would be in no condition to pack when I got back to my room. I had a cab coming at 7:00 a.m. to take me to Heathrow, so I packed before I left for the show.

I arrived at the theatre and saw Gavin walking off of his tour bus that was parked out front. We exchanged a hug and he invited me onto the bus for a drink. He poured me a glass of wine and told me about the ordeal his band had earlier that day at the French border.

Some of the other guys in Jaybird walked onto the bus and Gavin introduced us. They wanted to do shots of Jägermeister, which was not in my alcoholic vocabulary. I rarely did shots of Jäger for obvious reasons. But it was my last night in London, so why not?

After doing a round of shots, their tour manager, Russ, walked onto the bus. There was an issue with the venue. It was about 11:00 p.m. but another band was scheduled to go on before Jaybird. The promoter panicked when he heard Jaybird was held at the French border and booked another band.

"I don't want to pull a dick move and say we aren't going to play since it's our fault we were late," the singer said.

Another problem was that the Tube shut down at midnight. If they allowed another band to go on before them, most of their fans would miss their set to catch the last train home. They eventually let the band play, but cut their set short. And in order to be fair, Jaybird cut their set short too.

After solving that debacle, we went back to having cocktails. Gavin leaned against one of the tinted windows of the tour bus and pointed out two girls that were hanging out in front of the theatre. One was a cute, petite brunette. The other wore glasses and had wavy, pink hair pulled back into a bun. He said the girls were from Germany and had followed the band on the last few dates of the tour. He also mentioned they were at a Jaybird signing the night before and that the pink girl bit him. She was a bitch who was incredibly rude to their fans, and desperately wanted the band to hang out with her and her friend. That was the last thing Gavin and his band mates wanted to do.

There were other fans outside the bus, so the guys went outside to sign autographs and take pictures with whoever couldn't stay for the show.

Jaybird went on a half hour later. I followed them out of the bus and into the theatre where I ran into Raine. The crazy Germans followed behind me. They nestled themselves near the stage and started snapping pictures like they were paparazzi.

After the show, a crowd of fans hung around by the Jaybird tour bus. Raine took a few pictures with the guys and Gavin offered her a shot of Jäger, which she happily accepted. Off to the side, looming and overlooking everything were the crazy Germans. The pink bitch tried to muscle her way past a few fans to get to the singer. When he saw what she was doing, he blew her off. She put her tail between her legs and left with her friend, moments later.

Raine left shortly after the crazy Germans. I thanked her for taking me around London and sent her on her way with a shot of Jäger.

When I went back on the bus, I had a few more drinks and hung out with the guys. I thought an hour had gone by, but it was after 4:00 a.m. I quickly said my goodbyes and had Gavin call me a cab.

I got back to my room around 5:30. I was drunk and didn't have time for a power nap. I knew I would sleep through my alarm, so I took a cold shower, hoping it would sober me up.

I spent my last hour in London catching up in my journal. I was writing about my time at Abbey Road when my cab had arrived. I gathered my bags and stumbled down to the lobby.

I climbed into the cab and realized I had been up for twenty-four hours. Needless to say, I was exhausted. The driver said the commute to Heathrow was about forty-five minutes with traffic. I leaned my head against the window and passed out on the drive there.

I woke up shortly before the driver pulled into the airport. I sat up and realized I wasn't drunk anymore but still tipsy. I had to get it together to make it past customs. Thankfully, I did.

I drank coffee and splashed water on my face to keep me up. Neither had any affect on me. What I needed was a comfy bed. Instead, I found an empty seat near my gate I could nestle into. I wrapped both arms around my purse and fell asleep off and on for about an hour. I'm sure the people around me thought I was a junkie because I kept nodding off. I didn't care. My biggest concern was making that flight and keeping my purse safe while I slept.

When my flight was announced to board, I had never been so happy to see a coach, isle seat in my life. I hoped I was sitting in an empty row. That hope was dashed when a gentleman in his 50s kindly approached me and pointed to a window seat in my isle. Luckily, our middle seat was empty.

There's not much I can say about the flight back. I slept the entire way. The only exception being the two times the window seat guy woke me up to use the restroom.

I woke up as we descended into LAX. It was shortly after 1:00 p.m local time. I let out a big yawn and stretched my arms. The window seat guy let out a slight laugh and said he never saw anyone sleep that hard in his life.

Kenny from Blackboard Jungle and a few of the other old school kids were having a small barbeque that afternoon. Believe it or not, my intercontinental nap rejuvenated me by the time we landed at LAX. I went dropped off my things at home and went straight to the barbecue.

I sat by the pool, laughing at what a whirlwind the last twenty-four hours had been. Who would have guessed that only hours earlier, I was in London, screaming at a fellow American on Abbey Road?

Kenny walked over and said he was making a run to the nearest liquor store. I reached for my purse to give him money for a soda. Alcohol was the last thing I wanted. I opened up my wallet and it was filled with British currency.

I smiled and asked, "I don't suppose you take British pounds do you?"

# 7

# MAKING LEMONS INTO LEMONADE

*L*anding the job at Fireline was the beginning of many good things to come for me. Within a few months, I managed to pay off my car and save enough money to get my own place. After seven years of having a roommate, I was finally going to be alone. I couldn't have been happier.

One of the first places I looked at was near the Hollywood Hills. I didn't want to live in a stacked apartment building, so I was happy when I read there were only five apartments on the property. I made an appointment to see the place on my lunch break.

Boris, an old Russian gentleman, owned the property. He showed me a moderately sized one-bedroom apartment. I wasn't thrilled with it. I told him I would think about it and let him know.

"You not like apartment?" Boris asked in his broken English.

"I like it, it's just a bit small," I said, kindly.

"I show you other apartment," he replied before walking out the front door.

I followed him downstairs to another apartment. The first thing I noticed was how much light was bursting into the large, living room. It had glorious hardwood floors and crown molding along the ceiling and floor. The kitchen and bathroom were modest, but the bedroom was considerably large. I told Boris I wanted the apartment.

"Apartment is $1450," he said.

I didn't want to spend more than $1300, although I set my max at $1400. Even the smaller apartment he showed me earlier was pushing my limit at $1375.

"Oh no, really? I was hoping it would be closer to $1400. I don't know if I can pay more than that right now," I said, sweetly.

Boris asked what I did for a living. I told him about my new job and how I worked in the television industry. We spoke for almost an hour about the property, where I grew up and how he grew up in Russia. I hoped a good old-fashioned chitchat might convince him to drop the price on the apartment.

"Well, thank you for taking the time to show me the apartments," I said. "It's a shame this one is so expensive, I love it."

"You can pay $1400? Yes?" he asked.

"Absolutely. If I can get this place for $1400, I'll sign the lease right now." I replied.

"I ask wife first," he said with a smile and a slight laugh. "I call you later."

I drove back to work and made mental notes of where to place things in my new apartment. I hoped

Boris' wife would agree to drop the extra $50. Another concern was my less than desirable credit. The credit card that Jake and I shared a few years earlier had gone to collections.

Boris called me later that afternoon. His wife agreed to drop the cost of the rent! He also said I could move in whenever I wanted. We planned to meet at my new apartment the next day to go over my lease.

Boris asked about my credit when I met him the following afternoon. I was honest and told him I had a credit card that went to collections a few years earlier. He said as long as I didn't have any evictions or repossessions, he wouldn't need to run my credit. We went over my lease and he gave me the keys to my new place!

My priorities shifted when I moved into that apartment. It was also the first time I took notice of how much things had changed in my circle of friends. Long gone were the days of me being a teenager that bopped up and down the Sunset Strip. And I certainly wasn't the twenty-year-old girl stumbling around the bars of New York City with Pixie either. Most of the Sunset Strip kids I grew up with were getting married and having babies. Going out every night and getting drunk wasn't on our list of priorities anymore.

Without a man in my life, finishing my first book became my main focus. And believe me, I needed all the help I could get. I didn't know what the hell I was doing.

There were a million things to think about. Who would design the book cover? Should it be paperback, hardcover, e-book or all three? Do I include pictures? Who would be in the book? And most importantly, would anyone care to read it?

Before I addressed all of the above, I started with the basics. What was the point of my story? And how would it be different from any other book written about the Sunset Strip?

After doing some research, I found a common theme among most female-penned novels relating to the Sunset Strip. That being, most of the women were groupies or simply got caught up in the drug scene. Sometimes both. I'm not knocking anyone who had those experiences; we all have our stories to tell. But neither of those represented my point of view or the girls that I grew up with.

I never came to Hollywood with an agenda. I didn't care about being the most popular girl in the scene or bedding famous musicians. I was into glam rock music at a young age, which was dominant at the time and that's what brought me to Hollywood. My friendships were never based on popularity or trying to move up a social ladder. I wanted to show that you could come to Hollywood and not lose yourself if you kept a strong head and stayed true to who you are.

Another thing I noticed in several of those books were the inflated egos of the authors. I read several stories about friends of mine that I knew weren't true. I felt they were fabricated to make those women more of a Hollywood staple than they really were.

I wasn't going to lie about any events in my book, so I went one step further by including interviews. Not only with musicians, but more importantly, people I had conflict with. There are two sides to every story. I felt it would be a good contrast to show both perspectives, especially if their recollections didn't agree with mine.

Over the next several weeks, I drove around Los Angeles with my digital recorder. I conducted interviews with some of the guys in Glamour Punks, Blackboard Jungle, and Swingin Thing. Cassidy and

Dina agreed to be interviewed, along with a few others. I reached out to Dresden, but he didn't return my calls. Shocker.

After months of writing and interviewing my friends, I worked out a game plan for my first book. I found a self-publishing company that would suit my needs and a designer to create the artwork for my book cover.

I had a trunk full of live band photos I shot back in the day, but I chose not to include any pictures. The page count on my book was already over 300. I wasn't trying to write *The Iliad*. Instead, I created a Facebook page for the book and put the photos, along with my old flyers and other goodies in selected albums. At a later point in time, I hoped to compile them into a color scrapbook and sell it with my book as limited edition collector's set.

As everything slowly fell into place with my book, I realized I hadn't dated anyone in months. Not since Logan. The last time I had a serious boyfriend was almost a decade earlier. I suppose the thought of a relationship didn't weigh heavy on me, considering Pixie, Spencer and Cassidy were single too.

I didn't know where to meet a decent guy. I wasn't comfortable using a dating website. I also didn't like bar hopping either, and anytime a friend set me up with a guy, it usually resulted in disaster. I was fine being a single, 37-year old woman. And right when I adopted that mantra is when I met Eddie.

Spencer tried to hook me up with Eddie for months. She said he was sweet and we shared the same weird sense of humor. I met him once or twice before at various shows around Hollywood, but other than one of us screaming "hello" over loud music, we never had a real conversation before.

He was almost 6'4" with black dreadlocks and

light facial scruff. Despite his big stature, Spencer sang his praises and said he was one of the nicest guys I would ever meet.

I appreciated her efforts, but I wasn't biting. The last time I trusted a friend's recommendation, I ended up with Tyler, who was a borderline crack head.

But my biggest concern about Eddie? He was a musician, the singer of a metal band to be exact. I had been on both sides of the music scene, as a girlfriend and a friend. I wasn't stupid. I knew what went on behind the scenes, and I was too old to be heartbroken over a cheating, rock star boyfriend. I shared my concerns with Spencer and she assured me Eddie wasn't like other musicians. I hoped she would stop tugging on my ovaries at some point and hook him up with someone else.

While I dodged Spencer's matchmaking efforts, I watched another old school couple, CJ and Renee, take the marital leap into adulthood. They had a lovely wedding in San Diego that brought out many of the Sunset Strip kids like Mandie, Pixie, Cassidy, Spencer, and most of the Blackboard Jungle crew.

While I shook my ass on the dance floor with many of my old friends, I realized those special times where we could all get together were becoming few and far between. One exception being the yearly Blackboard Jungle reunion show. Back in the day, we knew we would run into each other every weekend somewhere in Hollywood. The biggest issue was getting a ride to wherever we were going. Now it was about finding babysitters and moving to a better school district for their kids. It was another slap of reality that we were all growing up.

After a crazy weekend in San Diego, I came home and took a hot shower. I was hung over from the wedding and wanted nothing more than to spend the night at home working on my book.

I was digging my ass into my comfy couch when I received a text from my buddy, Jay. He was filming a music video for his band at their rehearsal space that night and asked if I was coming to the shoot.

I was exhausted and looked like something that had been pulled from a clogged drain. The last thing I wanted to do was drive to downtown L.A. and be on camera. But I promised Jay weeks earlier that I would be in the video.

Spencer was supposed to meet me at the video shoot but she was running late. Aside from the guys in the band and one or two other people, I didn't know anyone else there. Then I saw Eddie sitting in a corner of the lobby on his iPhone. I bought my first iPhone a few weeks earlier. I figured I could use it as a topic of conversation and see where it went from there.

To my surprise, my conversation with Eddie flowed effortlessly. We talked about iPhones, our mutual friends, where we grew up and our thoughts on the paranormal. His big, beautiful blue eyes also mesmerized me. Maybe Spencer was onto something?

I was having a good time talking with Eddie when the director approached us. I don't know if he assumed we were dating, but he paired us to walk together in the video.

After we finished our scene, Eddie and I sat around chatting while we waited for the final group shot to be set up. There was quite a bit of downtime between takes, which left a lot of time for me to talk with Eddie. And the more we talked, the more I liked him.

We finished the final group scene sometime around midnight. I was gathering my things when I noticed Eddie walking toward the elevator by himself. I knew I wanted to see him again, so I jogged over to catch up with him.

I was having my birthday party the following weekend, so I invited him to come. When Eddie said he would go, my heart fluttered. It hadn't fluttered in years. After all the times my heart was broken, bruised, and punted in the air like a football, I didn't think it was capable of skipping a beat again.

The following weekend, Eddie showed up to my party and we hung out for most of the night. He even helped me pack up my gifts and put them in my sister's car. After things died down at my party, several of us walked down the street to the Rainbow.

I grabbed Eddie's hand and held it while we walked down Sunset Blvd. It was a bold move I never would have made on someone I just met. But there was something different about Eddie that put me at ease. He was sweet and engaging. When he spoke with you he looked you in the eye and gave you his undivided attention. I was never that comfortable around a guy before and ironically, it scared me.

Eddie's ride left without him. I told him he could crash at my place. Pixie was staying over too. When she and I went to the restroom to gossip, she said she would take the couch and let me have my bed with Eddie.

Despite being a little forward earlier in the evening, sleeping with Eddie was the last thing on my mind that night. I really liked him, and I wasn't going to ruin that by acting like a big whore on our first night out together.

After an hour or so at the Rainbow, Pixie, Eddie and I walked back to my place. I gave him some blankets and told him to holler at me if he needed anything. I left him on the couch and hopped into my bed with Pixie.

"Go out there and make out with him!" she

whispered.

"No I can't!" I said.

"Why not?"

"I'm scared!"

"Oh stop being a big chicken."

"I can't help it. I think I really like him."

"So go out there! And don't think about coming back in here until you've made out!" she said, ripping the sheets off of me.

I climbed out of bed and peeked into the living room. Eddie was wide-awake watching TV and lying under the blankets I gave him earlier. When I walked into the room, he smiled and my heart fluttered again. I walked over, curled up next to him on the couch and we snuggled as we watched TV. It was the strangest feeling I ever experienced, one that I never had before. It was comfort. He felt like home to me. I liked it and wanted more of it.

I started to fall asleep on his chest, and I could sense he was tired too. My couch wasn't comfortable for both of us, so I gave him a simple kiss goodnight, and hoped Pixie wouldn't throw me out of my room again.

A few days later, we went on our first date at a pub near my place. We had spoken a few times since the night of my party, and needless to say, I was excited to see him again.

There are few people I've met in my life that exude genuine, positive energy. Eddie was one of those people. While we sat there chatting, it hit me why I was drawn to him so quickly. It was his easygoing nature and sense of humor that reminded me very much of my father.

After our first date, Eddie and I started seeing each other on a regular basis. Although things were going great, a small part of me wondered if he was too good to be true. That's when a little piece of citrus put all my fears to rest.

Eddie and I met up with Spencer, her new boyfriend, and a few of our other friends at the Rainbow one night for dinner. The waitress brought over a few glasses of water and disappeared with our food order. I left my water untouched. I've never liked plain water, unless it has a splash of lemon in it. I know that sounds like a diva, but I really can't stand the taste of water. For some reason that splash of lemon makes all the difference, at least to me.

I planned on asking the waitress to bring some lemon wedges when she returned. I was cackling with Spencer when she returned, and I overheard Eddie ask the waitress for the lemon wedges. That's when my heart melted and I knew I loved him.

Yes, it was a stupid piece of fruit. But the fact that Eddie not only remembered something I liked, but cared enough to handle it without me asking? Well, that was selfless territory I hadn't encountered with any men I previously dated.

With Eddie, I could leave all of my emotional baggage behind. I never worried where he was or what he was doing. He was a man of his word. He was gentle without being a pushover, and he called me out on my shit in a way that didn't make me defensive. And the thing I loved the most about him? He was hilarious! There wasn't a day that went by where Eddie didn't make me laugh over the silliest things.

I eventually introduced Eddie to some of the Sunset Strip kids. They immediately fell in love with him. I even took him to a Blackboard Jungle reunion show. It wasn't his type of music; he's a metal head at heart. But he takes it all in stride and has a good time with everyone anyway.

Eddie was my biggest supporter when I fulfilled

the lifelong dream of releasing my first book. I titled it *Rock and Roll High School: Growing Up in Hollywood During the Decade of Decadence.* It was released in December of 2012. I had a private book release party in the downstairs lounge of the Viper Room in Hollywood, which he also helped me put together.

Before I met Eddie, I was the master of the two-year itch. None of my previous relationships made it past the second year. I usually started scratching to get out of them around the one-year mark. As it stands now with Eddie, we're going on almost three years together and I love him more with every passing day.

He was with me on the night of my dreaded 40th birthday. Surprisingly, it wasn't as tragic as turning 30. I originally planned on staying up until midnight but sometime around 11:30 p.m. we got tired and went to bed.

As I turned everything off in the living room, Eddie walked to the kitchen and asked if I wanted a glass of water. I said sure. When I heard the produce drawer open up, I smiled.

# 8

# EPILOGUE

*Then the last chord rang*
*And the crowd thinned out*
*There were no more anthems to shout out loud*
*Well, life settled in and we settled down*
*Sometimes she still misses that big drum sound…*

-MK4

*I* began writing this epilogue on the weekend of the latest annual Blackboard Jungle reunion show, the 11th in a row to be exact. What initially started as a small get together has turned into a yearly event that people plan their vacations around.

While the show is the centerpiece of the weekend's festivities, the partying starts well before the actual show takes place. People generally fly into Los Angeles earlier in the week. The days leading up to the show are spent barhopping, having dinner with old friends, and attending pool parties at various hotels along the Sunset Strip.

The reunion show has brought many old friends back into my life. It's also introduced me to several "new old friends" as I like to call them, which are people that ran in the same circles I did, yet never befriended until now. But as I mentioned in an earlier chapter, it's one of the few times where we can all get together. Not just for us locals that still live in Los Angeles, but for those that have moved across the country.

During the other 11 months of the year, I try to see my girlfriends as much as I can. But I find it gets harder as we all get older and life unintentionally separates us into different groups. Those that are married with kids tend to gravitate toward the other mommies and wives. The single girls want to go guy hunting with the other single girls, and yours truly who has a boyfriend is caught somewhere in the middle.

And while we're on the subject of life changes, I suppose this is where I should give you an update on everyone's whereabouts these days.

Pixie and Cassidy are industry professionals working the single circuit in Los Angeles. Britt is also single and moved back to San Francisco after Blackboard initially broke up. He teaches music to kids and plays in his other band, MK4, in his spare time. Joel, the drummer of Blackboard Jungle, is married and plays in his other two bands, Sky Parade, and David J and the Gentlemen Thieves. When he's not hopping between those bands, he runs his own vintage clothing store in South Pasadena called Moss and Ginger.

Kennedy, Amie and Dina are all married with kids along with Kenny and Dave from Blackboard Jungle, and Mandie from the Glamour Punks. Adding to the kids list are Chris and Sunny from Swingin Thing, and Spencer who had her first baby in early 2014. All are happy, healthy and living in Southern California.

My Turkish friend, Pandora moved back to Istanbul shortly after we stopped working on *Boston*

*Public*. She's married and had her first child in the summer of 2014. She hopes to move back to Los Angeles with her new family sometime soon.

Quincy, my other *Boston Public* alumni, also left Los Angeles and moved back to his hometown of Houston. He recently married his long time boyfriend and makes his living teaching musical theatre to kids.

My London mate, Raine, disappeared from her social media shortly after I returned from the U.K. But she's done that before. I hope to see her pop up in my newsfeed again someday.

Piper quit the management company she worked for and moved back to her hometown of San Francisco. She recently married and is looking forward to having kids soon.

When it comes to keeping in touch with exes, rebounds and everything in between, I don't have a set policy. Not all of them were bad. I deal with them on a case-by-case basis.

Ronan, for instance is someone I want nothing to do with for obvious reasons. I hadn't seen him for well over 15 years until he showed up at a Blackboard reunion show a few years ago. I left the moment I saw him. I haven't seen him since and I hope I never do.

Sheldon has been married and divorced since we broke up. He is single and living somewhere in the Midwest. He sent me a Facebook message not too long ago. He apologized for being a jerk and didn't remember how bad he was until he read my first book. I told him there was no hard feelings over what happened. Any colorful words I used were meant to express my feelings at the time and didn't represent how I felt now. I was also sorry to hear that his younger sister, Laney, has since passed away.

I haven't talked to Sebastian in quite a few years,

although we are Facebook friends. I contacted him about being interviewed for my first book but he never responded. He's now a Producer at one of Hollywood's largest movie studios. He also married another musician and continues to embrace the "Goth" culture.

Dresden still lives in New York and makes his living as a bartender. He's currently engaged, and his wife to be is a sweetheart. Eddie has met him and they get along famously. I think he likes Eddie more than me. I called him about being interviewed for my first book, but as I mentioned earlier, he conveniently dodged my calls. Shortly after the book was released, Cassidy told me he didn't agree with the way he was portrayed. He hadn't read my book yet but "heard" things through mutual friends that he wasn't happy about. Knowing me as well as she does, Cassidy told him he had no right to bitch. He had his opportunity to tell his side of things and didn't take it.

As for poor Karl, I never saw him again after we broke up. He sent me birthday cards for the first few years after we stopped dating. I felt so guilty.

Keith has been married and divorced a few times over the years and now has a girlfriend. He still lives in Arizona and we exchange a text about once a year or so to catch up on things. The Beat Angels have since disbanded, but Keith continues to play music in his other band, the Glass Heroes. He's also taken up acting and has landed roles in several small films.

I didn't see Dexter for well over a decade after we broke up. We started talking again after we bumped into each other at one of Blackboard's reunion shows. He sent me a Facebook friend request a few weeks later and I accepted. We drop a comment or a 'like' on each other's pages once in a blue moon, but that's the extent of our communication.

Jake and I haven't seen or spoken to each other

since he moved back to Omaha. I heard through a mutual friend that he's married with children and involved in the local theatre. I don't know what became of my *Star Wars* collection, and as a result I've stopped collecting. For all I know, it could still be locked up in that North Hollywood storage unit.

Andrew and I called each other a few times after he returned to New York, but we never spoke about continuing our romance. I wouldn't see him again until nine years later during a brief trip I took to New York. He had been in a terrible car accident a few months earlier and put on quite a bit of weight. But he was recovering with physical therapy and seemed to be in good spirits. We spoke like old friends and talked fondly of our brief time together in Los Angeles. I felt enough time had gone by to not have any awkwardness between us, so I had to ask what his issue was the night before he left Los Angeles. He said he ended a relationship shortly before landing the *Boston Public* role. He had a heavy conversation with his ex on his last day in L.A., which explained his detached demeanor when I arrived at his hotel that night. After hearing his story, I felt it was only fair I come clean too, so I confessed that I had a boyfriend during our first flirtatious weeks on *Boston Public*. We had a great dinner and it was fun catching up with him, but any sparks between us were long gone. I haven't seen him since our dinner, but we do stay somewhat connected through Facebook.

I bumped into Tyler at a mutual friend's party a few years after we broke up. He was tan and put on some weight. He finally looked normal since he was so damn skinny while we were dating. We had a friendly conversation, but I honestly didn't want to be around him. He was a reminder of a dark time in my life. That was the last time I saw Tyler. I heard he married an

Asian girl and still has the same crack head apartment in the Valley.

Believe it or not, Owen and I remain friends. He is single and still living in that glorious house on Lookout Mountain. I went to his last few birthday parties with Eddie, and they get along great. *Bridgepoint* was cancelled a few years after Owen left the show. It now runs in syndication on the TNT channel, and anytime I come across one of his episodes, I giggle to myself. That time frame always reminds me of us singing Journey and Carpenters' songs in his den on that karaoke machine.

Nick, my little folk singer, dated Holland shortly after we stopped seeing each other. But it wasn't long before they broke up and she stopped being the official 'band manager'. I haven't seen or spoken to him since we stopped dating. I'm assuming he still lives somewhere in Southern California. I continue to get emails about his upcoming shows in the Los Angeles area.

I don't talk to Ramone other than when I run into him, which is maybe once a year. He's dated several girls, including one porn star. I know his mood swings are still prevalent today by the amount of times he's activated and deactivated his Facebook account. I recently noticed he deleted me off of his friends list too. For what reason and when it happened, I don't know. I suppose I unintentionally boarded the "Ramonercoaster" without realizing it. He still lives in San Francisco and continues to play in Jumper. He makes his living as a Lyft driver.

Logan eventually came to his senses and broke up with the crazy girlfriend. We saw each other a few times after they split but only as friends. Vosbury also broke up about a year after we stopped dating. Logan now makes his living as a session drummer in various well-known alternative bands. He also has a side band with his new girlfriend. We exchange a Facebook comment here and there, but I haven't seen him in about three years.

Sadly, there were several people that didn't make it, along with Faye and Dizzy. Ronnie was one of them. He died in 2006 as the result of injuries sustained from a car accident. The last time I saw him was around 1999/2000 at the Dragonfly during the Pretty Ugly Club days. At that point, I hadn't seen him in about five or six years and there was talk that he had fallen off the wagon. When I saw him at the Dragonfly that night, I knew the rumors were true. He looked like a completely different person and was way too chatty. He also made a few rude comments about how I should have sex with Mandie, or as he put it, "*I really think you should fuck my buddy, Mandie.*"

In all the time I knew Ronnie, he never spoke to me like that before. I didn't know why he would say such a thing. Mandie and I were like brother and sister. Needless to say, his rude behavior pissed me off and I told him to go fuck himself.

We also lost another member of the Glamour Punks, Punk Rock Dave. I was never close with Dave, so I don't know the circumstances around his death. I only know he passed away sometime in 2011 if I'm not mistaken.

Drugs, drinking, and suicide claimed the lives of many other friends not mentioned in this book.

My days of bouncing around in clubs have slowed down considerably. But I've still noticed the changes in Hollywood's nightlife, and unfortunately, many of my favorite teenage haunts have seen their demise over the last twenty years.

The Coconut Teaszer was shut down in 2003 and replaced by Shelter Supper Club, which according to a few friends was basically a drug den. Shelter didn't last long and was soon replaced by a series of trendy clubs like Privilege and most recently, XIV. The property is currently being remodeled and will soon be the new location for Hyde, another trendy Hollywood club.

FM Station closed its doors in 1997 and has since been turned into a Spanish club called Salon Corona.

Gazzarri's officially closed in 1993. Hopes for it being taken over and reopened were dashed in 1994 following significant property damage from the Northridge earthquake. Billboard Live was built on its ashes and opened in 1996 but was shut down in 1998 and replaced by The Key Club, another live music venue. The Key Club had a good run until it closed in 2013. The property has since been transformed into a trendy dance club called 1Oak that opened in early 2014.

The Cat Club, which was two doors down from the Whisky, closed in 2011 to make way for an Irish pub called Rock and Reilly's. The same owners took over the neighboring property, Duke's Coffee Shop, a short time later. I used to go there for breakfast with Britt and the Blackboard crew the morning after their yearly reunion shows. Dukes was torn down in 2013 and replaced by a southern, 2-level speakeasy called Pearls. The owners of both bars recently acquired another neighboring property west of Reilly's. I hear they plan on knocking down that wall to expand Reilly's. The Whisky, Roxy, Troubadour, and Viper Room are going strong, although Johnny Depp gave up ownership for the latter in 2004.

The House of Blues on Sunset is rumored to move to another location in the next year or so. The current structure will be torn down to make way for a luxury hotel. This "facelift" of the Sunset Strip reminds me of the take over on St. Marks in New York, when the dive bars and historical music venues were shut down for franchise businesses and upscale living.

So much has changed that goes beyond the clubs on the Strip and the current style of music. The way musicians promote themselves and how we interact with each other is completely different now.

Bands don't pass out flyers or schmooze people at clubs to come to their shows anymore. There's no reason to when they can sit at home and do the same thing with a digital flyer that can be posted online. There are no more hand-written fan letters, only emails and comments on social media pages. And gone are the days of rushing to your local record store to pickup your favorite artists' new album. That experience has been replaced by digital downloads.

The one peace of technology I haven't adjusted to completely is the e-book. Sure, I'll have my books available in e-book form, but I can't bring myself to read one on a tablet. I love the feel and smell of holding a book in my hands. I'm just biased I suppose.

One of the questions I get asked the most since the release of my first book is, "If you could relive those days on the Sunset Strip all over again, would you?"

Honestly, I don't think I would. Yes, I had a great time back then. I met a lot of amazing people; many that I'm still friends with to this day. But aside from the parties and gallivanting around the boulevard, it was hard. It was hard being a young girl in that scene. Granted, you are who you surround yourself with, but when you're a teenager you're also a victim of your age group. I don't know many 18 year olds that choose to hang out with an older crowd because they're tired of the immaturity that comes from their circle of young friends. There is a certain level of drama and stupidity that you can't get away from when it comes to peers in a young age group. I had my fill during the Sunset Strip days and a few years afterward. Now that I'm 40, I feel all my ducks are in a row, both personally and professionally. I have a great job, an amazing boyfriend, and I've long since weeded out all the stupid people in my life. I'm well aware of the namedroppers and leeches that circle around Eddie and I in Hollywood. We keep a small group of friends and that's who you'll see us spending time with, rather than raging at wherever Hollywood's latest hotspot may be.

So after that long-winded filibuster, my answer is no. I wouldn't do it all over again. I feel that whatever good or bad times I've gone through in the past have put me in the good place I'm at today.

It is interesting how that scene has found its place in a whole new generation. Since the release of my first book, I've received messages from kids, wishing they could've experienced those crazy times on the Sunset Strip. They even dress the way I did back then, and these are kids that were born around the time I graduated high school. But I suppose it's no different from the kids I went to school with in the '80s who were dressing like hippies and wished they were alive during the days of "flower power".

Do I miss those times? Absolutely. But another reason why I wouldn't relive them is because they wouldn't be special to me if I did. They wouldn't be special to any of us if we could redo those precious moments in our lives over and over again.

So what is the key to happiness?

In my opinion, it's keeping an open mind. You have to be open to change. That's what life is all about. Life is going to hand you amazing things you could never have imagined. Other times, it will shove its foot so far up your ass that you'll be coughing up shoelaces. Regardless, you have to keep an open mind to change because it's inevitable. This is a lesson I was challenged with recently as I completed work on this book. I reluctantly accepted that a once close friendship of over 20 years was drifting into the acquaintance zone, and there was nothing I could do about it. It was disheartening, but sometimes people change and you grow apart for whatever reason. You have to let change happen and keep moving forward.

People, relationships and jobs will drift in and out of your life for a reason. Rather than trying to hold onto the past, you should let it go. I truly believe it's life's way of making room for something better that's just around the corner for you!

Keep reading for a preview of:

# CRAZY PARTY OF ONE:
## The Sane Woman's Guide to Dating in Los Angeles

# COMING SOON!

Visit www.marisatellez.com for details.

# 1

# First Impressions

*F*irst impressions aren't everything but they do hold considerable weight. In my 25 + years of dating in Los Angeles, I've learned one universal thing about men that comes standard like having fries with a burger. Men have a short attention span.

Taking that into consideration, I suggest you treat your first date like a pitch meeting. Make your points clear, concise and leave out unimportant details. You don't want to be a 'Chatty Cathy'. Nothing loses a man's interest more on a first date than a woman who talks his ear off, so practice some self-control and know when to shut yourself up. If you want to tell your potential love interest about a great dinner you had the other night, then get to the point and tell him why it was great. He doesn't need to hear about the road rage you encountered on the way to the restaurant or the great pair of shoes you bought that day. Save the bitching and extra curricular cackling for your girlfriends.

You should also avoid talking about your past relationships. Treat it like the head of Medusa. Don't look at it and don't talk about it! It's a sticky situation that could turn a casual conversation into a therapy session before your appetizer arrives. You'll have plenty of time later on to dive into each other's past history. But on the first date, I suggest not bringing it up at all or if you must, tread lightly and with extreme caution.

First dates are exciting but you don't want to come off as being too eager. One of the biggest complaints from my male friends is when a woman plans their future activities before they've finished dinner, so take it back a notch. Chew your food twice as much as you normally would and give your date space to breathe and contribute to the conversation. Dessert should be an option. You don't want your date paying the bill while swallowing their last bite of dinner because they're trying to get the hell away from you.

When it comes to picking out an outfit for your first date, always consider the 'hooch factor'. Looking sexy is one thing. But dressing up like you're about to twerk at a club in Miami during spring break is a whole other issue. I'm not saying to slip on a burlap sack and a burka, but there's a fine line between sexy and trashy. If you have an ample physique, you might want to consider tucking in your tits and saving the apple bottom jeans for another time. You want your date to take you seriously and that's highly unlikely if you have your casaba melons spilling out of a low cut top and onto your dinner table.

# Other books by Marisa Tellez:

## ROCK AND ROLL HIGH SCHOOL
### Growing Up in Hollywood During the Decade of Decadence

# AVAILABLE NOW ON AMAZON WORLDWIDE!

Visit www.marisatellez.com for details.

13499926R00132

Printed in Poland
by Amazon Fulfillment
Poland Sp. z o.o., Wrocław